CW00961772

We are Mayo

Tom Brett Sean Rice

Published by: Tom Brett

ISBN: 978 -1 - 5272 - 5490 -9

Design and layout: Jacinta Reilly, KPS Colour Print, Knock, Co. Mayo
Printed by: KPS Colour Print, Knock, Co. Mayo

Cover Images:

Front Cover Image:
The traditional Mayo jersey worn by Eamonn Brett making his Mayo debut at right half back in the 1974 All Ireland minor final loss to Cork.

Back Cover Image:
Dun Briste Aurora (Photo: Brian Wilson)

Contents

Contents

Section 4 People and Places

Section 5 Sport

Section 6 Music, Song and Mayo's Dark Skies

About The Authors

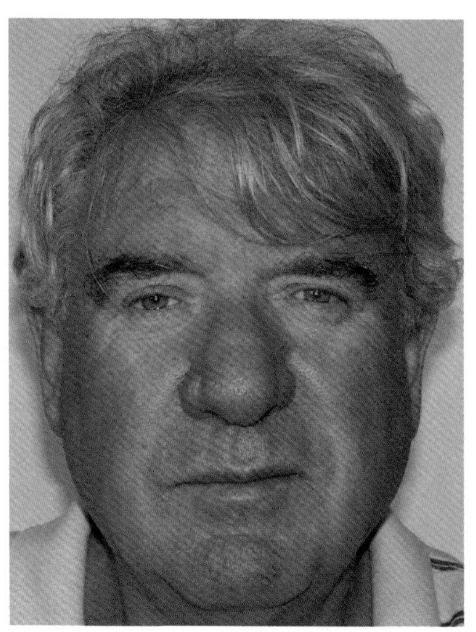

Tom Brett

Tom Brett is a native of Charlestown and currently lives in Fremantle Western Australia. He is a frequent visitor to Ireland especially his home county of Mayo. He was educated at Lecarrow National School, Rockwell College, St Joseph's Secondary School Charlestown and University College Galway (NUIG). After completing BA and MA degrees, he switched faculties graduating in Medicine in 1979. He moved to Australia in 1984 where he now works as a general practitioner and in academic general practice. He is currently professor and director General Practice and Primary Health Care Research at The University of Notre Dame Australia in Fremantle. On the sporting front, he represented Charlestown and UCG in gaelic football and won All Ireland Inter-Firm medal with Western Health Board in 1983. He has also represented UCG, Galwegians and Connacht in rugby.

Sean Rice

A native of Castlebar, living in Islandeady. Educated at St Patrick's NS and St Gerald's College Castlebar. Holds a diploma in Social Action from UCG. Joined the Connaught Telegraph as general reporter in 1965. Eight years later, joined the Connacht Tribune based in Tuam. Involved in all aspects of journalism including sports and a general column written under the title "Western Diary." Having retired from the Tribune he commenced writing a weekly sports column for the Mayo News which he continues to pen each week. Edited history of Castlebar Mitchels GAA and Westport GAA Clubs. Won Connacht GAA Council sports coverage awards with the Tribune and Mayo News. He is a lifetime member of the National Union of Journalists.

Dedications

To my daughters, Deirdre and Sarah; grandchildren Holly, Madeline, Mitchell and Finley; my parents Patrick and Katie Brett for the gift of life, and to my sister, brothers and extended families.

To Pauline, Marina and Adrian without whose support this would not have been possible.

PHOTO ACKNOWLEDGEMENTS

The authors acknowledge the support of the following with photos for the book

- Mayo.IE, Neil Sheridan
- Mayo County Council
- Mayo County Library, Maureen Costello
- Anthony Hickey
- Michael Donnelly
- Failte Ireland
- Westport House
- Mayo International Dark Skies
- Brian Wilson
- Liam Lyons Collection Mayo County Library http://www.mayolibrary.ie/en/LocalStudies/PhotographicArchive/
- Fidelma Lyons
- Achill Tourism
- Mayo North Tourism
- Mid-West Radio
- Western People
- Mayo News
- Connaught Telegraph
- Fergus Sweeney / Sweeney Family Collection
- Ceide Fields OPW
- Religious Sisters of Charity Foxford Woollen Mills
- Ireland West Airport Knock
- Donal Healy
- Knock Shrine
- PM Photography and AD Wejchert Architects
- Oliver Whyte
- John Michael Nikolai
- Eamonn De Burca / De Burca Rare Books
- Anne Chambers - Copyright the biography of Margaret Burke Sheridan, 'La Sheridan: Adorable Diva' by Anne Chambers
- Dom Greally / Tooreen GAA Club
- Orla Loftus
- Westport Golf Club
- Ballinrobe Golf Club
- Ballina Golf Club
- Ballyhaunis Golf Club
- Admiral William Brown Society Foxford
- Brendan Brett
- Oliver Murphy
- Brendan Graham
- Michael and Ethna Viney
- Gretta Byrne
- Joe McGowan
- Eamon Delaney / Delaney Family
- Johnnie O'Malley
- Fr Peyton Memorial Centre Attymass
- Brisbane Archdiocese
- Armagh Archdiocese
- Clare Island Lighthouse
- Michael McLoughlin
- Davitt Museum Straide
- Alan Johnson, Swinford Photography
- Una Leavy
- Anne-Marie Flynn
- Alison Crummy
- Nephin Beg Photography
- National Ireland Visual Arts Library, National College Arts and Design
- Shea Tomkins
- Michael Ring
- Rose Kenny
- Kate Gibson
- Kevin Finnerty
- Gerry O'Donnell
- Michael McGing
- Robert Brett
- Daphne Haire-Mooney
- Margaret Flaherty
- Derek Dempsey
- Padraic Walsh
- Maureen Moore
- Joan O'Gara
- Christy Loftus
- Henry Kenny
- Eamonn Brett
- An Post / Anne O'Neill
- John Fallon

FOREWORD

Sabina Higgins

FOREWORD – SABINA HIGGINS

Mayo to me is primarily the place of my early years – my childhood and youth, the years of my formation. It is family, place, nature, school, church religion, songs, books, and storytelling – stories from books and from life. Mayo to me is my memory of my childhood, schooldays in Ballindine National School and Claremorris Secondary School.

The endless treasure of poems in Irish and English and speeches from primary and secondary school are among my most precious possessions which I still so enjoy reciting when some association throws them up, out of the blue, into my mind, as Beckett says they remain "to help me through the day".

The time was spent around the home, the farm, the townland and the small town or village, and a bigger town for secondary school and once a year the children's day at Knock when one saw children and uniforms from schools all over Ireland.

Ballindine the town – other places called it 'the village', was one broad street – almost as "broad as Balla" that had about eight shops, four of which were pubs and general grocers, a school, a church, a priest's house, doctor's dispensary, a post office, and a Garda barracks. Boys' and girls' schools shared the same two-storey building and playgrounds with a wall dividing them. I have happy memories of walking to and from school with my sisters and neighbouring children.

Religion dominated much of our lives and accounted for the big occasions – Sunday Mass and monthly sodality with confession. It accounted for the big occasions of the First Communion with white dresses and veils.

I have a memory of Confirmation with mine and my sisters' dresses spread over the chairs in the kitchen ready to be put on, the morning sunshine shining in on them through the back window. The Corpus Christi procession was a big occasion, when all the people of the area went up through the town to the tree, which had been transformed into an altar, the priest himself covered by a canopy and people carrying sodality banners. The houses of the town were decorated with altars of roses, lilac rhododendrons, and broom, and rockets and peony roses.

The people all assembled at the tree altar for benediction and then all went back through the town to the Church – the children in their communion dresses and veils strewing flower petals from decorated baskets, and the women wearing blue Children of Mary cloaks and white veils, singing hymns like The Bells of the Angelus which sounded so special and wonderful in the open air, being carried by the breeze.

Rural electrification was only being installed during this time, so I remember dark evenings lit up by the oil lamp, later by the wonderful Tilley Lamp, with its white mantle and lovely smell of methylated spirits and the beautiful light it gave which compared well with the electric light when we had the great occasion of its switching on, and we had the magic of light in every room just by pressing a switch on the wall.

The bicycle was the great treasure as there were very few cars and the need for one for very special occasions was supplied by the one hackney or a lift from a cousin maybe.

There was no television and just a periodic showing of a film in the old Town Hall or an even rarer occasion on a Sunday when one cycled to the cinema in Claremorris. Films were a big deal, mostly cowboy films – Roy Rogers on his Hi Ho Silver Away – and Gene Autry – great films like Shane, Magnificent Obsession and Random Harvest.

I had, in one way, the most idyllic of childhoods. In summer we girls did not play any sports, and there was no television so, my time was my own. I could spend my time reading, which I did to excess, day and night and wanted nothing more. I lived and laughed, suffered and wept with all those fictitious people in the great classics and some-how they became real. They have all remained part of me. Reading is still the greatest source for my imagination and is still such a great joy.

Having the great privilege of growing up on a farm, I had all the pleasures and excitement of experiencing the agricultural season. Spring with the soft primroses and violets on the hedges. The little lambs gambolling around in the fields and bleating for their mothers, and the ewes feeding from the troughs. I remember calves being born and the lovely curds and whey from the cow's new milk.

I remember the ploughing, Daddy and Jack Cleary, his brother-in-law, with whom he was in was in co-operation for ploughing, bringing the horses together and turning up the brown clay as they guided the horses and ploughed the fields for putting in the crops, the oats, the wheat, the barley, and the potatoes that my mother would cut into slits so there was an eye in each, and would have scattered with lime so the worms would not eat them.

It was a joy cycling up to the bog to bring gorgeous big sandwiches of homemade bread and fried bacon and eggs to Daddy and my brother Colm, and seeing the turf being cut and spread on the heather and footed into grógin and then cruacáns, later to be brought home in the cribbed carts to be made into a rick beside the house. Later still being carried in brusheens or put into homemade sallyrod skibs, made by my father, for the fire.

The seasons were so clear on the farm. Walking through the long grass of the meadows. The cutting of the meadows with the beautiful horse-drawn, McCormack mowing machine, then the saving of the hay, the shaking, the turning, the raking, the making of the haycocks and then the bringing in, by horse-cart to make the big haycocks in the high garden or into the hayshed.

There was the beautiful sight of the fields of oats or wheat as they went golden and were cut with the scythe, tied into sheaves and made into stooks and brought in to the high garden, until the excitement of the day that the thrasher came. All the neighbouring men - the meitheal, came to feed the thrasher, holding the bags for the beautiful grain and storing it in wooden chests in the high barn and leaving the big stacks of straw in the garden.

It was lovely going out with my mother and sisters, and the cats coming too, when she milked the cows in the fields in summer and in the cow-house in winter. Always singing as she milked them or telling us the stories of books – like Dickens – that she had read; always finishing by dipping her fingers in the milk and touching the cows back hip in a kind of thanks or blessing as she finished, and left the lovely warm smell of the cow-house and the hay.

Out in the fields there was the thinning of the turnips and the carrots and parsnips to allow some to grow big. The picking of the potatoes at the end of autumn which was one of the few tasks in which we children joined. The potatoes were picked, put into buckets and brought to a potato pit, that had been dug in the field and lined with rushes or hay. When it was full and a few feet above the ground it was covered with hay and rushes, and then covered with clay to save as a store and to be free of frost.

Coming home from October devotions meant playing around on the road with the other children while mammy and aunt Ellie and the women from The Mountain and Cloonmore stopped to chat in the bright moonlight.

Hallowe'en was an exciting time, full of stories of puckies and ghosts, games of ducking to bite an apple in a bucket of water or caught from being suspended on a twine.

I love history as the narrative of our lives and I am so proud and inspired by the great part Mayo has in that history. It was so exciting to have been at the various commemorations. Mayo had suffered so much during the Famines of

1845-1847 and 1879-1880, Mayo people are so rightly proud of Michael Davitt and the Land League. It was such a great occasion when the centenary commemoration was held in the same field in Irishtown - just 3 miles up from Ballindine- where the first great public founding meeting was held. They are proud of the success of the Mayo strategy of "Boycotting" in the Land Agitation as a resistance to eviction.

I was also so pleased that Michael and I were able to attend all the great commemoration events of the Bicentenary of the 1798 Rebellion where the focus was on the rising in Mayo – The Year of the French commemorations were held in Kilcummin, Killala, Castlebar, and Westport, and for the inauguration of John Moore of Moore Hall as President of the first Republic of Connacht.

So, Mayo to me is the place where I grew up and spent my childhood and early years. It is a place so very different from the Mayo in which a child of today grows up. Nowadays I continue to have a lot of contact with Mayo, and my brother, nephew and nieces and their families all live happily there.

Though I seldom see any of my classmates from secondary school now, other than when we had a day in Áras an Uachtaráin together, they are all still as clear to me, and dear to me now as they were then, and are still a part of me. It seems like as though one keeps bonded to those classmates from primary and secondary school for life.

Dwelling now on the happy memories, Mayo means an idyllic, dreaming childhood, which had a reality all its own. I lived there until I was seventeen and looking back that now seems like a wonderland to me.

I wish a happy childhood to all the present-day Mayo children.

My hopes and wishes are always and remain for a happy future for County Mayo and all its people, now and in time to come.

President Michael D Higgins and Sabina

INTRODUCTION

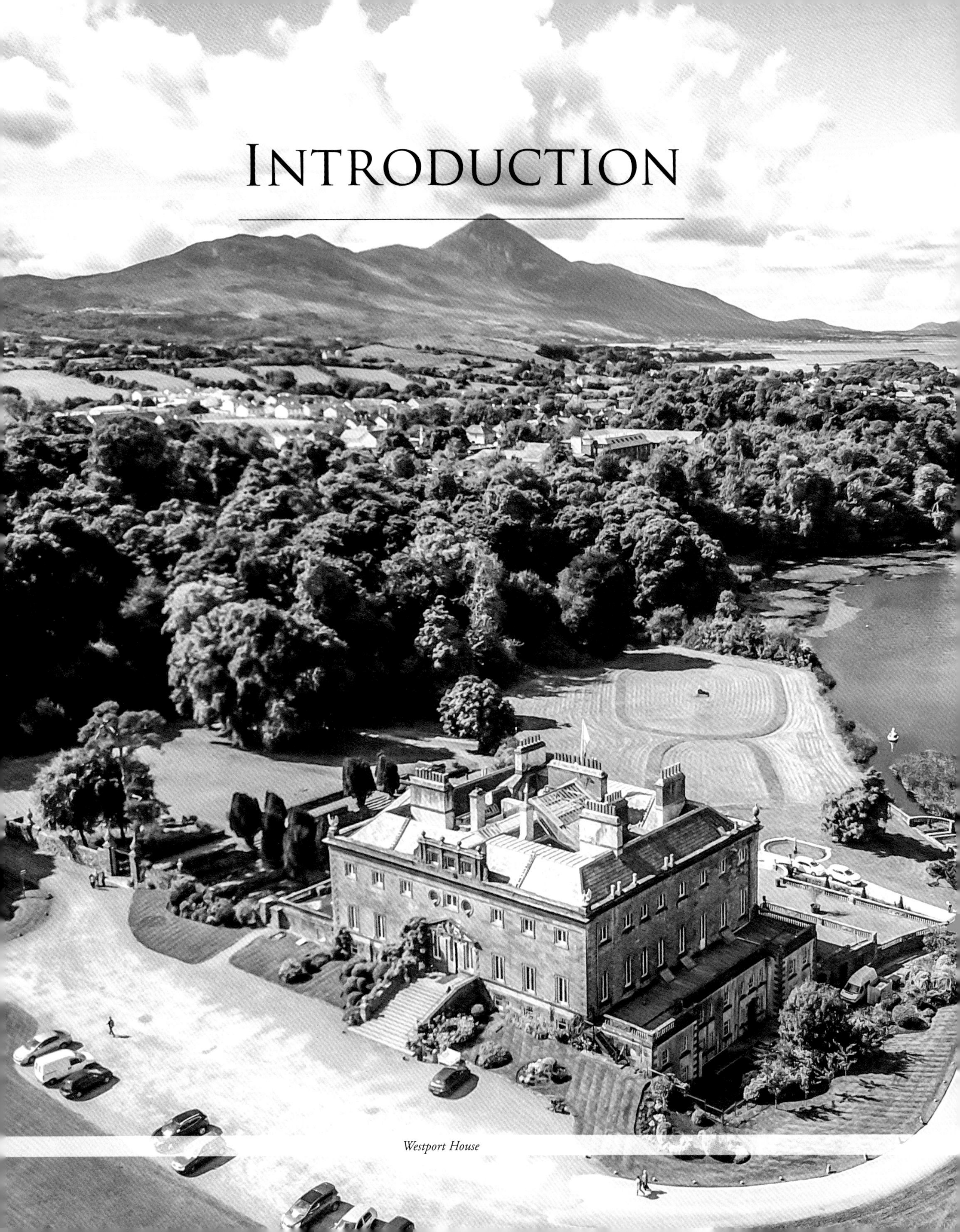

Westport House

INTRODUCTION

Located on the west coast of Ireland, Mayo is the third largest county on the island of Ireland and widely regarded as one of the most scenic and least spoilt of its natural beauty. It forms one of the five counties of the province of Connacht and is bounded to the north-east by Sligo, to the east by Roscommon and to the south by Galway. To the west and north of Mayo is the great Atlantic Ocean, with the nearest landfall being the east coast of North America. New York is over 3,000 miles (5,000 kilometres) away over our western horizon.

The history and geography of Mayo add to the allure of the county for visitors and natives alike. In Irish, Maigh Eo means 'plain of the yew tree' with the county taking its name from the village of Mayo Abbey, near Balla. The current population of the county is just over 130,000 inhabitants with Castlebar and Ballina forming the two largest towns and Westport showing increasing growth.

Dun Briste Downpatrick Head (Tom Brett)

The Great Famine of 1844 -1849 had a devastating effect on a largely rural Mayo population at the time. The 1841 census recorded Mayo's highest population ever at a staggering 388,000 – three times the current population. The horrible effects of blight coupled with a population over 90% of whom were dependent on the potato as their staple diet, brought death and emigration from Mayo on an unprecedented scale. Thousands died from starvation. Those fit enough to emigrate sought to make their way mostly to England, Scotland, Wales and the United States.

Sixty years later in the 1901 census, Mayo's population had halved to 199,000. The next 70 years covered the period of two world wars, economic recession and depression but little economic growth for rural west of Ireland. By 1971, the migrant route continued to be Mayo's safety valve and that year's census showed a new low with a population of just 109,000 inhabitants.

In the 1970s, Ireland joined the European Common Market and economic and social benefits to Mayo gradually began to show benefit. In addition, education policies in Ireland, especially free secondary education, free school bus travel for rural communities and grants to attend university, had a powerful impact both psychologically and strategically. Suddenly, the opportunities for third-level education opened-up and talented students could pursue emerging careers hitherto inaccessible to most families. Rural communities kept their students at home for the summer. They could now field football teams and compete equally in key competitions. Mayo families saw their children develop their career paths locally with the opportunity to continue to live their lives in their own country.

Mayo's population just about held its own in the twenty years to 1991 when that year's census recorded a population of 110,00 for the county. Then the Celtic Tiger economic boom kicked in and Ireland started to record net immigration. Outbound travel was for holidays to Europe, the United States, Canada and Australia and other exotic locations. The European diet of pasta, pizza and wine encroached on the more traditional Irish bacon and cabbage menu. European travellers returned home with cars stocked with wine and other delicacies from our continental neighbours. Suddenly, by 2011 Mayo's population had grown to 130,000.

The economic and social benefits from our new European partnership brought significant changes to the emerging Irish economy and infrastructure development gradually spread to County Mayo. New motorways were developing with a focus of the eastern seaboard while Knock Airport confounded all the doubters by its resounding success.

There is a lot of merit in strategically placing an airport towards the centre of an island country such as Ireland. Whilst shipping must have its coastal ports, aircraft need clear air space, a good road network and easy access. No wonder Mayo's near neighbours in Donegal, Cavan, Monaghan and Fermanagh find Knock Airport should a treat for their overseas travel. The lack of quality motorway to Mayo west of Mullingar remains a major drawback.

Our county is packed full of treasures that we are happy to share with our visitors. This book is about us, Mayo people, and those of you who would like to share in the joys of what Mayo has to offer. Sit back, relax and enjoy the journey together. We are Mayo!

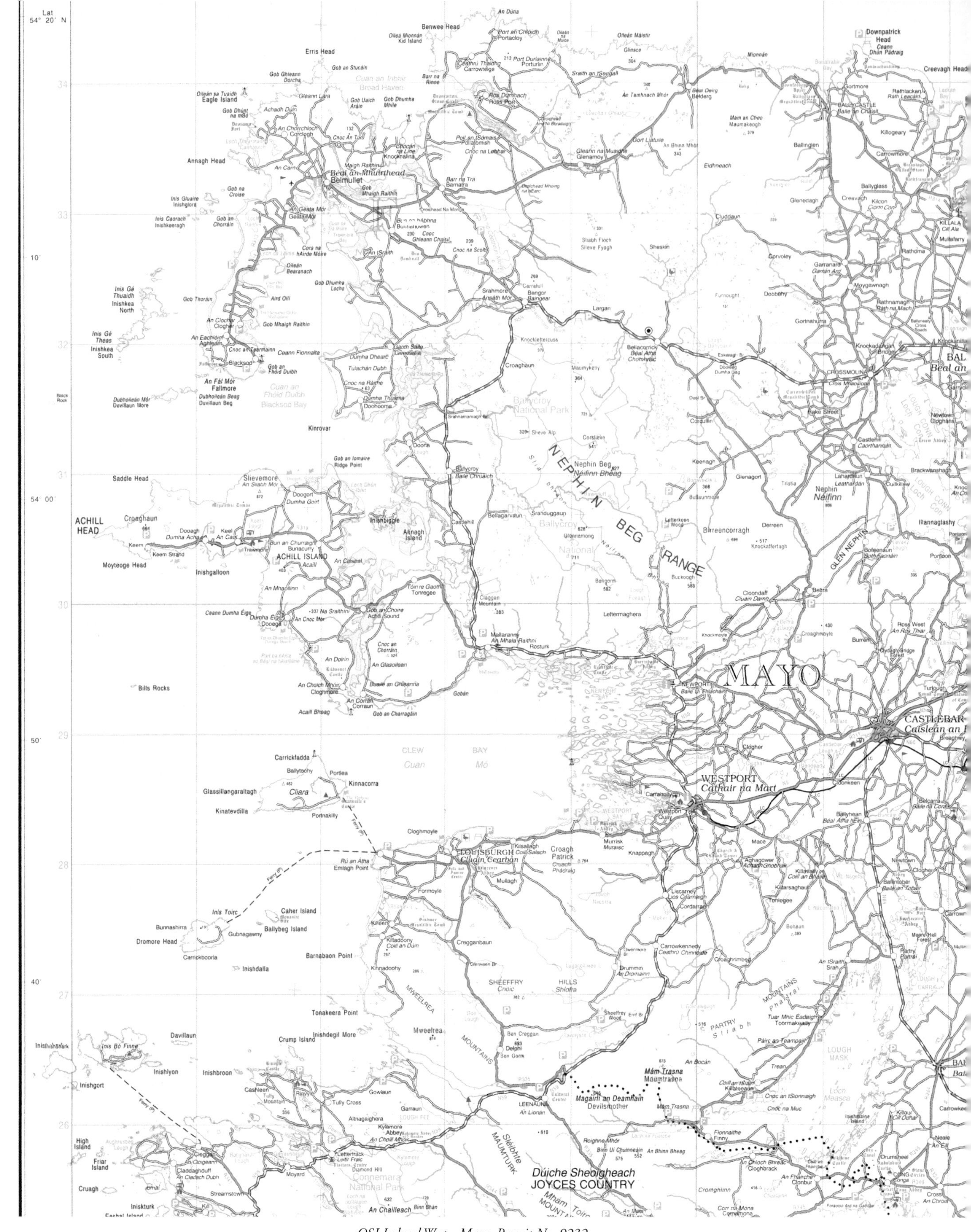

OSI Ireland West - Mayo Permit No. 9232

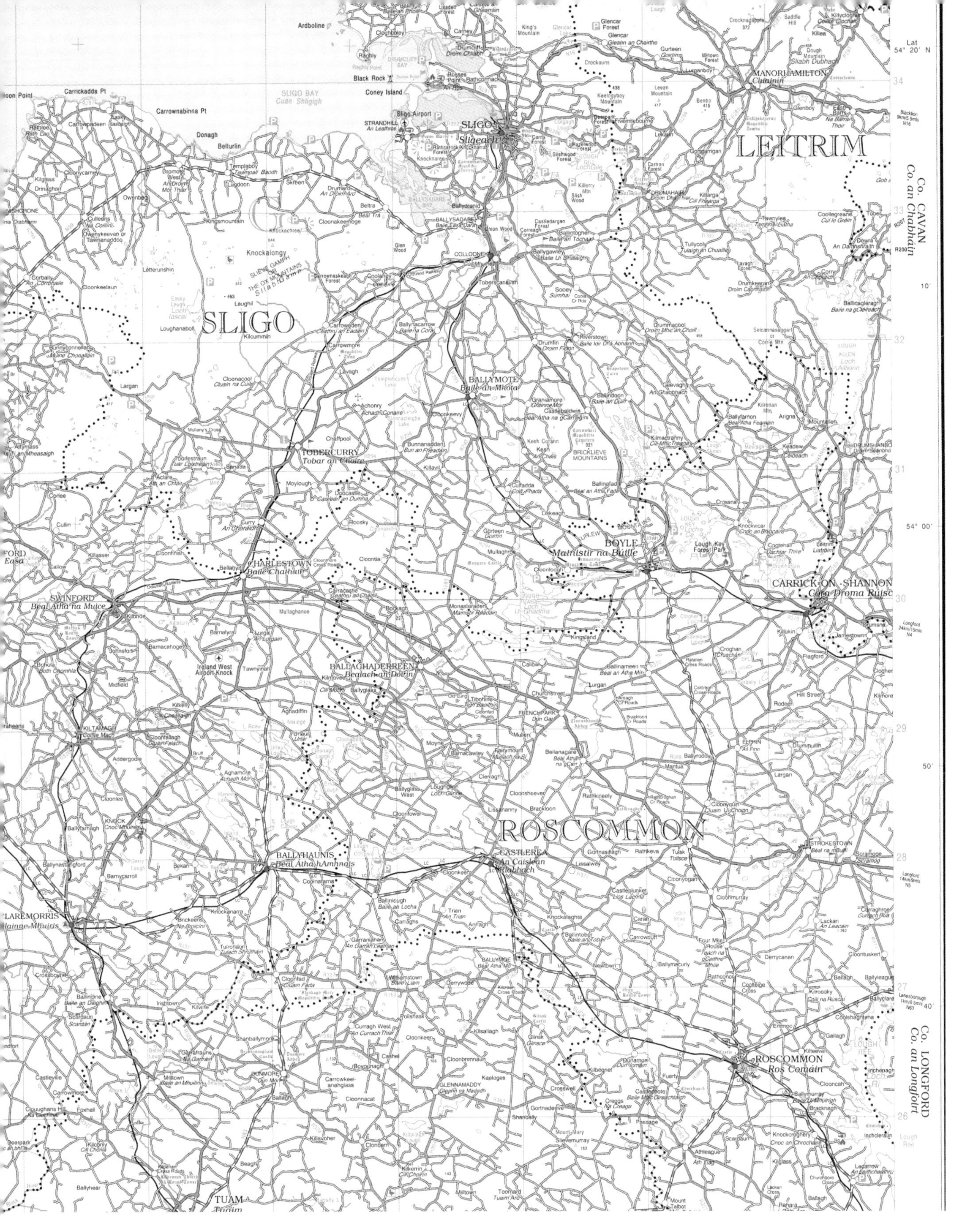
SLIGO
LEITRIM
ROSCOMMON
Co. CAVAN
Co. an Chabháin
Co. LONGFORD
Co. an Longfoirt
SLIGO BAY
Cuan Sligigh
SLIGO
Sligeach
STRANDHILL
An Leathros
Sligo Airport
MANORHAMILTON
Cluainín
DROMAHAIR
BALLYSADARE
COLLOONEY
BALLYMOTE
Baile an Mhóta
TOBERCURRY
Tobar an Choire
CHARLESTOWN
Baile Chathail
SWINFORD
Béal Átha na Muice
BOYLE
Mainistir na Búille
CARRICK-ON-SHANNON
Cora Droma Rúisc
DRUMSHANBO
BALLAGHADERREEN
Bealach an Doirín
FRENCHPARK
Dún Gar
ELPHIN
Ail Finn
KILTAMAGH
Coillte Mach
KNOCK
Cnoc Mhuire
BALLYHAUNIS
Béal Átha hAmhnais
CASTLEREA
An Caisleán Riabhach
STROKESTOWN
Béal na mBuillí
CLAREMORRIS
BALLYMOE
GLENNAMADDY
Gleann na Madadh
DUNMORE
Dún Mór
ROSCOMMON
Ros Comáin
TUAM
Tuaim
Lat
54° 20′ N
10′
54° 00′
50′
40′

SECTION 1

GEOGRAPHY

Road to Keem Bay (Photo: Failte Ireland)

MOUNTAINS

As a county with an international reputation for walking, trekking and mountain climbing, it is not surprising that beautiful mountains form a very prominent part of the Mayo skyline. Mweelrea is the highest peak in Mayo and in Connacht, closely followed by Nephin and Croagh Patrick – the latter rightly regarded as one of the iconic tourist markers for Mayo and the west of Ireland.

Mweelrea (814 metres) can be accessed either from the Doolough Pass to its north or from the Silver Strand area to the south. Climbers are advised not to undertake the trek to the summit of Mweelrea if weather conditions are poor and visibility is limited. On a good day, the mountain offers some spectacular panoramas over Killary Harbour, **Maumturk** mountains and the **Twelve Bens** to the south, the **Sheffrey Hills** to the north and **Ben Gorm, Ben Creggan, Maumtrasna** and the **Partry** mountains to the east. On the Atlantic western side, the panorama includes Inishbofin, Inishturk, Achill and Clare islands. Outdoor adventure activities, fishing and accommodation are available in the Dephi area, Leenane and Louisburgh.

Mweelrea Mountain (Photo: Tom Brett)

Climbing **Croagh Patrick** (764 metres) can be challenging and is not for the faint hearted. A few people sadly perish each year on Ireland's holy mountain and care should be taken to recognise your limitations if you are feeling in an adventurous mood. Each year thousands of people undertake the pilgrimage on the last Sunday in July while the feast of the Assumption on 15 August is another busy climbing day. But don't be surprised to encounter hundreds if not thousands of people on the mountain on any fine summer's day.

Croagh Patrick from Westport Quay (Photo: Tom Brett)

A good policy is to follow the weather forecast for the area and make sure you can see the little white church on the summit before starting out. Hopefully you will get there in about 90 minutes to 2 hours with the final 300 metres of the cone the most challenging. It is a good idea to plan to take a rest especially after you have summited above the ridge and the terrain becomes flat, even downhill, for a short while. The wind can be quite strong approaching the ridge so light, layered clothing should be the order of the day to deal with the elements. Fluids and some food for energy replacement will encourage you to rest a while and enjoy the vast expanse of Clew Bay with its 365 islands and the impressive Clare Island further out to sea.

There is nothing more welcome than the sight of that little white church once you reach the summit of Croagh Patrick. A few journeys around the church enhances the spectacle and you get to meet others more than welcome to share their experience of the climb and backfill you with information of where they've come from and where they're heading. Mayo people encourage their visitors to be good conversationalists and this endearing feature can be a good source of information especially for other places and sights not to be missed on your travels.

The trip down the mountain can be hazardous too with the scree of the cone causing many falls especially if moving too fast or from being too adventurous. The joy of getting down safely, closing the gate at the bottom and circling St Patrick's statue to salute his 40 days and 40 nights at the top back around 441 A.D., should be enough to encourage you to seek some sustenance in one of the many local pubs and restaurants in Murrisk or Westport. And celebrate all the plenary indulgences you will have accrued into the bargain!

Nephin Mountain (Photo: MAYO.IE)

A snow-covered Nephin Beg - part of Wild Nephin - Ireland's first designated wilderness area. (Photo: Anthony Hickey / Mayo.ME)

Nephin (806 metres) is situated close to the Crossmolina to Castlebar road near the village of Lahardane. While not the most elegant mountain in the county, it nevertheless offers some great views of the surrounding countryside including Lough Conn to the east and Crossmolina and Erris to the north. There are various climbing options including ascent from north of Lahardane and descent through the centre part of the mountain. The terrain tends to be wet and boggy with little in the way of defined paths. Wellington boots can often be a better option than traditional walking boots… A cairn marks the summit and a chance to rest, enjoy some food and fluids, and pick out the prominent landmarks. On clear, sunny days views over the Ox mountains and Sligo as far as Slieve Leigue and Errigal in Donegal have been reported. As usual, the descent should be approached with caution and never in haste.

Sunset over Nephin (Photo: Tom Brett)

One of the most scenic areas in County Mayo is that occupied by the **Nephin Beg Range**. Starting out from Castlebar and talking a leisurely drive on the R311 in the direction of Newport, take a turn to the right towards Beltra on the R312. After you pass Beltra Lough on the left there are some excellent vantage places to stop and enjoy the everchanging scenery. Beyond Beltra you should continue on the R312 towards Bellacorrick passing Nephin on your right. To the left, Birreencorragh (698 metres) and **Nephin Beg** (627 metres) followed by **Corslieve** (541 metres) will come into view.

At Bellacorrick, you should follow the N59 as far as Bangor before turning left southwards towards Ballycroy and onto Mulranny, with excellent coastal and mountain scenery throughout the journey. Achill island will be to your right. To the left will be **Glennamong** (627 metres), **Claggan** and **Bengorm** mountains. You are now entering Mayo Dark Sky country – an area rapidly developing an international reputation among star-gazers and astronomers alike because of the clarity of its light-free skies and rugged hinterland.

The area includes both the Ballycroy National Park and the Wild Nephin area, both famous for the opportunities offered to experience glorious and idyllic night-time viewing of nature in its purest and rawest forms. In recent years, Mayo's International Dark Sky area has achieved 'Gold Tier' status.

Achill island boasts some of Mayo's highest peaks and finest coastal scenery. **Croaghaun** (688 metres) lies at the end of the road and towers above Keem Bay while **Slievemore** (671 metres) near Doogort offers panoramic views northwards towards Blacksod, Iniskea North and South as well as Doohooma.

As you complete your journey from Mulranny to Newport and back to Castlebar you will have circumnavigated the entire Nephin Beg Range. The area is very popular with national and international walkers with the Castlebar International Walking Jestival every July now over 50 years in existence.

Croagh Patrick and Rodney (Photo: Oliver Whyte)

Erris and north Mayo are relatively flat with **Slieve Fyagh** (320 metres), **Benmore** (348 metres) and **Maumakeogh** (377 metres) between Belderrig and Ballycastle, the most prominent. While most of the **Ox mountains** lie to the north east of Mayo in County Sligo, there are parts in County Mayo between Attymass and Bonniconlon.

The Ox mountain area around Foxford and Attymass offers some terrific walking trails and, after summiting the crest, some stunning views are available in all directions. The pride of Mayo's modern infrastructure, Ireland West Airport, is visible on the horizon to the south. To the east, the Windy Gap and Lough Talt areas on the Ballina to Tubbercurry Road offer particularly spectacular scenery.

Addergoole Titanic Memorial Park (Photo: AM Flynn)

Curraun Hill (Photo: Oliver Whyte)

MALIN HEAD
CIONN FHÁNADA
Buncrana
City of Derry Airport
Donegal Airport
Dungloe
DERRY
Letterkenny
Port of Larne
Belfast International Airport
Belfast Harbour
Belfast City Airport
BELFAST
SLIABH LIAG
Donegal
MULLAGHMORE
DOWNPATRICK HEAD
Sligo
Belmullet
Ballina
KEEM BAY
Ireland West Airport Knock
Westport
KILLARY HARBOUR
DERRIGIMLAGH
Clifden
Dublin Airport
Dublin Port
DUBLIN
Dun Laoghaire Harbour
GALWAY
Connemara Regional Airport
Doolin
CLIFFS OF MOHER
Lehinch
Shannon International Airport
LIMERICK
Kilkee
Kilrush
Foynes
LOOP HEAD
Ballybunion
Tralee
RADHARC NA MBLASCAOIDÍ
Dingle
Kerry Airport
Killarney
Rosslare Harbour
Waterford Airport
BRAY HEAD
Waterville
Sneem
Kenmare
CORK
Cork International Airport
Cork Harbour
Kinsale
Castletownbere
Bantry
Clonakilty
DURSEY ISLAND
Skibbereen
OLD HEAD OF KINSALE
MIZEN HEAD

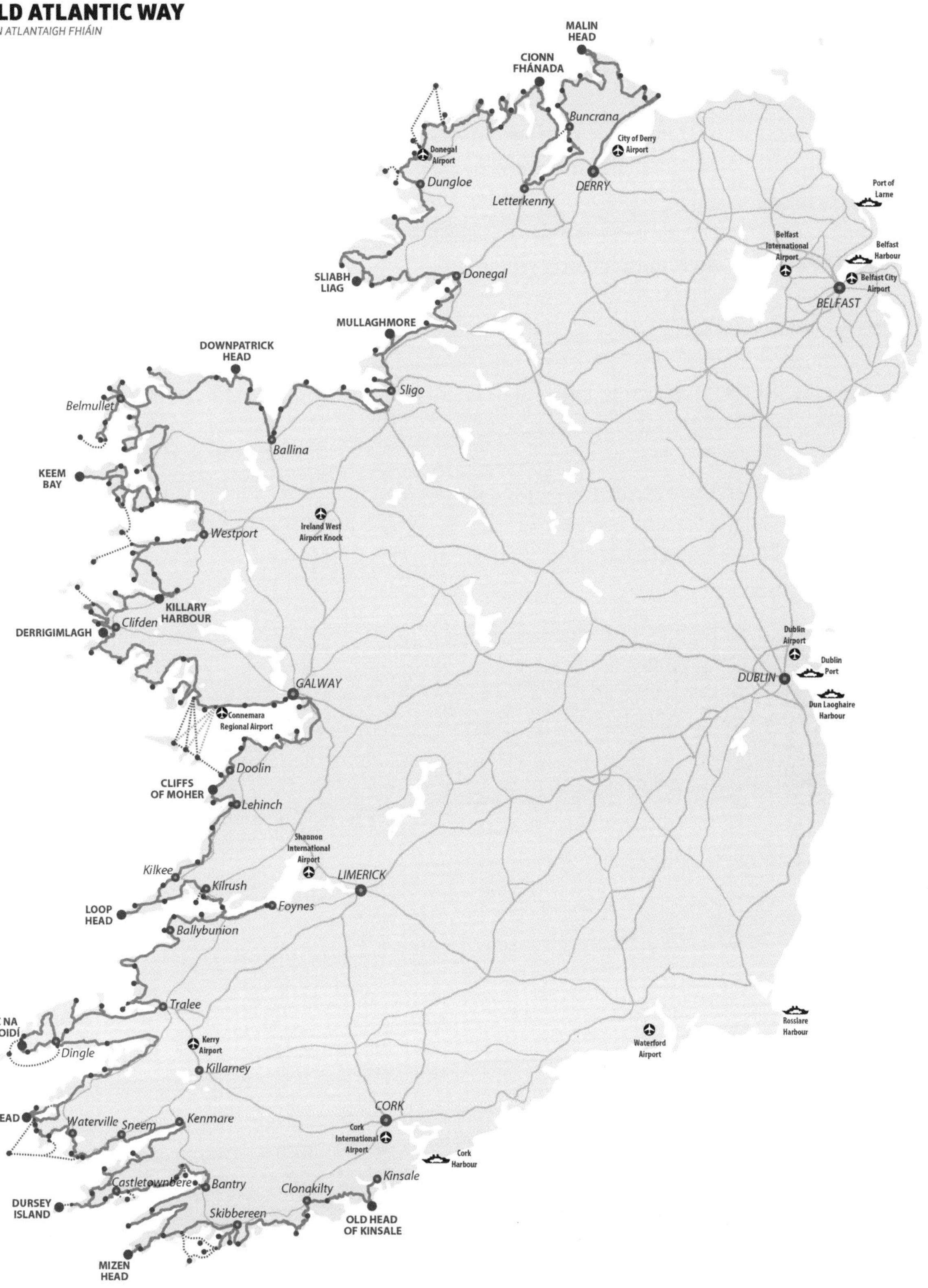

Wild Atlantic Way Map (MAYO.IE)

ISLANDS

Mayo's coastline faces onto the broad Atlantic Ocean stretching from Killary Harbour in the south up to Erris Head in the north and then eastwards as far as Killala Bay. The Wild Atlantic Way stretching from West Cork in the south of Ireland to Donegal in the north is now world famous for the quality and beauty of its scenery. It is best undertaken at a reasonably leisurely pace especially through some of the spectacular coastal areas of County Mayo. Better still, take an even slower route with some deviations to have a closer look at some of its islands.

Just north of Killary Harbour and some 14km from the shore lies **Inishturk** (island of the Wild Boar). There are regular ferry services to Inishturk throughout the year. These depart from Roonagh Point beyond Louisburgh and are much enjoyed by day-trippers who get a chance to enjoy the circular walking loops, some beautiful coastal scenery and golden, sandy beaches.

The local community centre and pub at the top of the hill provide the necessary sustenance and relaxation while bed and breakfast accommodation is also available for those with time to linger that little bit longer. The night time entertainment and craic at the pub can be lively too! The Tale of Tongs sculpture offers a new and exciting dimension to your trek around the island.

Inishturk looking East (Photo: Tom Brett)

Inishturk towards Croagh Patrick (Photo: Tom Brett)

Inishturk Coastline (Photo: Oliver Whyte)

Further north from Inishturk is the larger **Clare Island** that is dominated by Knockmore rising majestically to the west. On a fine day, one of the finest views of the island is on approaching Westport from the Castlebar side when Knockmore suddenly pops into view in all its glory. Clare Island is serviced regularly by two ferry companies and tends to be busier than Inishturk with lots of accommodation including a hotel, pub, bed and breakfasts as well as the more luxurious Lighthouse facility on the northern fringe opposite Achill.

The island has a long association with the 16th century pirate queen Grainne Uaile (or Grace O'Malley). Apart from her maritime plunderings, Grainne Uaile is also famous for sailing up the Thames to strike a deal with fellow royal, Elizabeth 1. The local population on Clare Island is about 130 but this number can treble in peak holiday times. There are limited cars on the island allowing the opportunity for leisurely walks and sightseeing. Vantage points on the island allow the opportunity to look eastward towards the mainland with Croagh Patrick in the distance; southwards towards Inishturk and Inishbofin and north towards Achill, Newport and Mulranny.

Clare Island roadway (Photo: Oliver Whyte)

Clare Island sunset (Photo: Oliver Whyte)

Clare Island pathway (Photo: Oliver Whyte)

Clare Island Harbour (Photo: Oliver Whyte)

Road to Slievemore (Photo: Achill Tourism and Failte Ireland)

Achill Island is the largest of Ireland's offshore islands. It is now joined to the mainland by a bridge at Achill Sound. It is a favourite holiday destination and a popular haunt for nature lovers, walkers and hikers as well as painters and writers. The island is dominated by the solid Croaghaun mountain as well as the majestic Keel Bay. Visitors will never be short of places to see or capture on film – a deserted village on Slievemore near Dugort, giant sea cliffs, the picturesque villages of Dooagh and Doeega as well as Grainne Uaile's Kildavnet castle on Achill Sound.

Keem Bay, Achill (Photo: MAYO.IE)

But the greatest gem on Achill Island and sometimes not experienced by the unaware, is the beautiful Keem Bay, literally at the end of the road. Many visitors who come to Achill and are not well acquainted with its geography may not realise that this delightful oyster shaped bay lies down a twisting road at the end of their journey. A swim and a stroll in Keem Bay should be a must do for every Achill visitor. It will draw you back again on your next trip, this time with friends in tow for all to enjoy its beautiful, tranquil water and picture postcard location.

Keem Bay Achill (Photo: Failte Ireland)

In the shadow of Achill Island and located just off Ballycroy is the small inhabited island of **Innishbiggle**. Currently, it has just 19 regular residents down from 162 in 1926. The island is serviced in its own unique way with small boat ferries, either from Doran's Point, Ballycroy with Michael Leneghan as your captain or from Bullsmouth, Dooniver in Achill. In fine weather, access by boat is easy but in stormy weather the sea currents between Achill and Innishbiggle along the Bullsmouth Channel can be extremely dangerous.

The island has a shared inter-denominational church for both Catholic and Protestant faiths. There is no school or pub on the island and a packed lunch is an essential part of your day's visit to experience the local scenery and island life. An added bonus for visitors to the island is the nearby Ballycroy Dark Sky area where star-gazing and peaceful solitude come hand in hand.

On the western, Atlantic side of the Mullet peninsula lie the two **Inishkea islands**, north and south. The name Inishkea (Inis Ge is the isle of geese) reflects the Barnacle geese that travel thousands of miles from their summer home in far off Greenland to enjoy the solitude of remote island life off the Mayo coast for their winter season.

After a tragic storm in October 1927, which resulted in the loss of ten islander fishermen, the remaining inhabitants questioned the long-term viability of their perilous existence. In the 1930s the island homes were finally abandoned and have remained uninhabited since then. Despite this the islands are still visited by descendants and friends of the islanders and by holidaymakers who want to enjoy some of the joys of island life.

Just north of Inishkea lies the small island of Inishglora mostly famous for providing the final Mayo chapter in the mythical Children of Lir fable.

The ruined dwellings on Inishkea South, abandoned by islanders in the 1930s, ending 4,000 years of habitation on Inishkea South and North, located off the Mullet. (Photo: © Anthony Hickey / Mayo.ME)

Atlantic Drive Achill (Photo: Failte Ireland and Achill Tourism)

Achill Scenic Walkway (Photo: Failte Ireland and Achill Tourism)

RIVERS

A night scene at Ballina Quay along the banks of the River Moy. (Photo: Anthony Hickey / Mayo.ME)

The **River Moy** is synonymous with County Mayo's tourist industry and ranks as the premier salmon fishing river in Ireland. The Moy rises in the foothills of the Ox Mountains in County Sligo roughly mid-way between the villages of Cloonacool and Coolaney before emerging as a small stream to cross the main road at Branchfield village. It then flows in a south-westerly direction through the village of Cloonacool, onwards through Benada, Cloonfinish, Kilasser and Cloongullane bridge on the Swinford to Foxford road. At the village of Kilmore near Straide, the Moy takes a sharp northernly turn progressing on this path through Foxford and Ballina to enter the sea in an expansive estuary near Enniscrone at Killala Bay.

The 100 km path of the Moy is dominated by the Ox Mountains hugging its northern bank on its winding, U-shaped journey from County Sligo. The flatter terrain approaching Foxford allows it to take advantage of the disappearing mountains and take its northerly route to the sea. Lough Cullin and Lough Conn border and link to the Moy on its western side in County Mayo with both lakes benefitting from the rich supply of salmon and trout through the river's link to the Atlantic Ocean.

Salmon fishing is one of pearls of Mayo's tourism industry and attracts increasing worldwide popularity. International celebrities, including the former Irish International soccer manager, Jack Charlton, have enjoyed the rich fishing on the river for many years. The close location of Mayo's Ireland West Airport Knock near Charlestown helps too with transfers less than an hour away.

Drift net fishing at the mouth of major rivers such as the Moy had caused serious damage to fish stock in the region prior to the practice being outlawed in 2007. Since then, fly fishing for salmon has seen a resurgence with places such as the Rock Pool in the Moy's estuary in Ballina drawing increasing numbers of visitors to the county to test their skill and luck on the river.

Tributaries of the Moy also boast good trout and some salmon stocks. The Owengarve (or Curry) river, the Mullaghanoe and Sonnagh rivers all enter the Moy in the Ballinacurra area while further west the Pollagh and Glore rivers unite to form the Gwestion river near Bohola. Further west, the Clydagh river rises in the Nephin Beg range before joining up near Ballyvary with the Castlebar river and the Manulla river to flow into Lough Cullin as the Ballyvary river. In Ballina town at 'The Point', the Moy is joined by the Brusna or Bruree river as its last major tributary.

The Deel river, whose origins are nearly 30 miles away in the Nephin Beg Range, flows eastwards through Crossmolina before emptying into Lough Conn. In recent years the Deel has been subject to significant flooding with large parts of Crossmolina becoming inundated at times due to heavy downpours of rain along its journey to Lough Conn.

The River Robe rises between Claremorris and Ballyhaunis and journeys westward through Ballinrobe before emptying into Lough Mask. Rivers in this limestone area can sometimes disappear underground such as occurs with the Black River that forms part of the Mayo-Galway border and flows through Shrule village en route to Lough Corrib. There is an underground link between Lough Mask and Lough Corrib while the Cong River canal is subject to seasonal vagaries in the watertable.

Aasleagh Falls (Photo: Tourism Ireland)

The Erriff river flows in the valley between Maumtrasna and Ben Gorm / Ben Creggan mountains before tumbling into Killary Harbour. The Aasleagh Falls on the Erriff river can offer spectacular sights when in full flow after recent rain.

Photographic opportunities are a key part of many of Mayo's river basins – so always travel prepared for unexpected vistas!

The Carrowniskey river which rises near Mweelrea and the Owenmore river that flows through Louisburgh, both flow westwards to the sea. The Owenree river is west of Westport while the Carrowbeg river provides some scenic charm to the town centre. Further north, the Black Oak / Newport river empties waters from Lake Beltra through a large estuary at the port in Newport. The towering arches of the former Westport to Achill railway line over the river in Newport provide a stunning backdrop for your personal memento of your visit to the area.

Other westward flowing rivers in north-west Mayo include the Owenduff which enters the sea north of Ballycroy and the Owenmore river formed by the confluence of the Oweninny and Altnabrocky rivers at Bellacorrick. The Owenmore is quite a substantial river that flows through Bangor Erris before entering the sea at Tullaghan Bay. Further north the Glenamoy and Muingnabo rivers both empty into Sruwaddacon Bay and offer abundant sea trout and salmon fishing.

Newport Night (Photo: Brian Wilson)

The beautiful Briska waterfall near Bangor Erris. (Photo: Anthony Hickey / Mayo.ME)

Lakes

Lough Mask is a world-renowned limestone, trout fishing lake located in the southwest of County Mayo. It is roughly 10 miles long and 4 miles wide and is positioned between Lough Carra to its north east and Lough Corrib to the south. The limestone terrain ensures many of these lakes are inter-linked with Lough Carra emptying into Lough Mask, which in turn is linked by an underground river that emerges as the River Cong and ultimately flows into Lough Corrib. Waters from these three lakes flow into Galway Bay between the Spanish Arch and the Claddagh in Galway City.

Every year thousands of fly-fishing enthusiasts converge on the Ballinrobe / Cushlough Bay area of Lough Mask for the World Cup trout fishing competition. The lake is an ideal breeding area for trout with the wild brown trout from the lake regarded as the best in Ireland. The area and water content of Lough Mask is vast – the second largest lake by water volume on the island of Ireland and the sixth largest in size. Whilst the eastern parts of Lough Mask are relatively shallow, there are much deeper areas (up to 80 metres in parts) on the western flanks. In warm summers, the water table is known to drop by up to 3 metres in some areas due to the porous limestone terrain.

Lough Corrib, which is predominantly located in County Galway, has a relatively short frontage onto County Mayo between Cong to the north and almost as far as Headford to the south. Visitors to Lough Corrib and the Cong area will be familiar with the majestic **Ashford Castle** located just outside Cong on the banks of Lough Corrib.

To the north of County Mayo, **Lough Conn** and **Lough Cullin** are two large fishing lakes that boast considerable stocks of trout and salmon. Lough Conn is linked to the River Moy through Lough Cullin, this vital sea link helping to replenish its rich salmon stocks. The picturesque village of Pontoon sits on the narrow piece of land through which the river linking the two lakes flows. Lough Conn lies in the shadow of Nephin (806 metres) which offers outstanding views of the lake and the surrounding countryside.

Other lakes in County Mayo include **Carrowmore Lake** (6.5 km long and 5 km wide) lying between Bangor and Barnatra in the north west. It is generally regarded as the best spring salmon lake in the county, also possessing a plentiful supply of wild brown trout. Nearer Newport, other good salmon and wild brown trout lakes include **Lough Feeagh, Furnace** and **Beltra Loughs**. East Mayo has numerous smaller, trout fishing lakes with Urlaur lake between Ballyhaunis and Kilmovee and **Callow** lakes outside Swinford two of the largest. Callow has a reputation for good quality wild brown trout.

Lough Conn reflecting Nephin (Photo: Nephin Beg Photography)

Anglers catching the last rays of sunlight fishing from the shores of Lough Conn at Pontoon. (Photo: Anthony Hickey / Mayo.ME)

SECTION 2

INFRASTRUCTURE

Airline [illegible] ng[illegible] and Ryanair (IWAK)

LIGHTHOUSES

Few structures define and reflect the history and geography of a country quite like its lighthouses. As a coastal county with a large exposure to the great Atlantic Ocean along its western and northern fringes, Mayo has many tales to tell of fateful days and events from times in the near and distant past. Because of their strategic locations and their colourful marine background, lighthouses often present themselves as places of iconic beauty and historical significance.

Eagle Island lighthouse (Photo: F Sweeney)

Eagle Island lighthouse (54.28 degrees North and 10.1 degrees West) off the north-west tip of Mayo stands at a point where the Irish coast makes a ninety-degree turn. It has thus always been a key player because of its strategic location. Prior to the establishment of Knock Airport, many aircraft used Eagle Island as a focal locational aid in their travels.

When first commissioned in 1830, Eagle Island had two lighthouses separated by 120 metres of land. There were built to a height of 67 metres above sea level with visability in fine weather as far as Blacksod Bay to the south and Broadhaven Bay to the east. They cost 40,000 pounds sterling to construct in the early 1830s and became fully operational in September 1835. The lighthouse stands a further 60 metres above the high-water mark.

The constant pounding from wild Atlantic storms coupled with the island's position at the edge of the Continental Shelf inevitably comes at a cost. One of the two original lighthouses was destroyed in a fierce storm and was never repaired. In the mid-1800s, local accommodation had to be provided for the lighthouse keepers and their families and a total of seven dwellings were recorded on Eagle Island in the 1841 census. Seventy years later in the 1911 census, just a single dwelling is recorded there.

Records of storm damage include a rock breaking a window twenty-seven metres high up the lighthouse tower in January 1836 while a rogue wave in March 1861 broke 23 window panes and flooded the tower to such an extent that the lighthouse keepers were forced to drill holes at the base of the structure and clear the water to gain admission.

They make them hardy off the north-west coast of Mayo but eventually it was decided to de-commission the living quarters for families on Eagle Island. Families were re-housed at Corclough in the 1890s and keepers were rotated to the lighthouse. Finally, on 31 March 1988, a decision was made to make the lighthouse automatic and keepers were no longer required to stay there.

Black Rock lighthouse and flying gull (Photo: F Sweeney)

Black Rock Island lighthouse (54.1 degrees North and 10.3 degrees West) lies about 12 miles off Blacksod Bay to the north-west of Achill island. It rises to a height of 70 metres above sea level and was constructed in 1864. It is the most westerly lighthouse off the Mayo coast and one of the most remote in Ireland. The local rainfall is heavy – about 72 inches per annum.

The lighthouse consists of a single-storied keeper's house and a 50-foot tower painted white. In 1974 Black Rock became automatic and the island lost its only inhabitant. Solar power was introduced in 1999. The keeper of Blacksod lighthouse on the mainland beside Blacksod pier has responsibility for maintenance of its neighbour with helicopter now the preferred mode of travel.

Black Rock Lighthouse has had its share of drama over the years. One of the resident lighthouse-keepers, Patrick Monaghan, was lost to the sea in September 1937. In August 1940, a German bomber attacked and dropped some bombs on an Allied ship, SS Macville, causing some damage to the lighthouse roof and broke a few of the panes on the lantern.

Severe storms during the winter of 1942-43 meant that three lighthouse keepers became stranded for extended periods. Their plight was not helped by emergency rationing in force at the time due to World War 11. Walter Coupe endured 117 days and Michael O'Connor 90 days isolated on the lighthouse. A few attempts were made by boat to supply provisions. Some were partially successful before a lull in the weather enabled successful evacuations and replacements. More recently, the tragedy of the crash of an Irish Air Corps helicopter into Black Rock on a night-time rescue mission on 14 March 2014 resulted in the deaths of four Irish Air Corps personnel.

View Termon Hill to Blacksod pier, lighthouse and bay (Photo: F Sweeney)

Blacksod lighthouse (54 degrees North and 10 degrees west) is located at the southern tip of the Mullet Peninsula, close to Blacksod pier. Work on the lighthouse commenced in 1864 and the fortress-like structure built with high quality reddish-grey granite quarried from the local Termon Hill was deemed ready for the installation of its lantern in the summer of 1865.

The contract for the lantern was awarded to the Chance brothers of Birmingham and their previous work included many fixtures for lighthouses around the world including Low Head in Tasmania as well as glazing contracts for the Houses of Parliament, the Crystal Palace in London and the White House in Washington. The official opening of Blacksod lighthouse took place on 30 June 1866. After commissioning, it showed fixed red and white light which has remained in constant use ever since to help guide mariners safely into Blacksod Bay.

Blacksod Lighthouse (Photo: Tom Brett)

Blacksod Lighthouse (Photo: F Sweeney)

Blacksod lighthouse is unique in many ways apart from its square, rather squat structure at the end of the peninsula. Currently only the lantern section at the highest point of the building is painted white. Records show proposals to paint the entire building in the traditional white lighthouse colour but the general consensus is that this never really occurred and the natural reddish grey granite has kept its own precious colours since construction. The two-storey building includes quarters for the lighthouse keeper and family. The lighthouse was converted to electricity on 31 May 1967 and this was augmented with a back-up diesel generator in case the electricity supply failed.

Ted and Maureen Sweeney (Photo: Sweeney Family Collection)

The legendary lighthouse keeper associated with Blacksod is Ted Sweeney who was first appointed to the position of Attendant on 1 November 1933. Since then, his son Vincent and grandson, Fergus, have continued their association with the lighthouse. Ted became a local, national and international hero during the Second World War through his other duties in supplying local weather information from the Mullet Peninsula to Dublin.

Prior to the D-day landings in Normandy in France in 1944, Ted and his Blacksod Post Office clerk, Maureen (from Knockanure in North Kerry and later to be his wife), provided on the spot advice of weather conditions at Blacksod and this local Mayo knowledge proved pivotal in the Allies exploiting a window of opportunity that the Germans did not foresee. The Allies moved on Ted and Maureen's information and the rest is history. Ted also looked after the local Post Office and between 1969 and 1972 it operated out of a room at the lighthouse while repairs were undertaken.

In July 1969, an English trans-Atlantic rower, Tom McClean, who had hopped into his boat 70 days earlier in Newfoundland, pulled into Blacksod after an epic voyage across the Atlantic. I'm sure he was glad to get his land legs back again and probably enjoyed some refreshments for his troubles with the locals.

Ballyglass or Broadhaven lighthouse (54 degrees North and 10 degrees West) lies at the opposite end of the Mullet Peninsula at the entrance to Broadhaven Bay. The lighthouse building was constructed in 1848 with the lantern commencing operations on 1 June 1855. The light was visible for about 20 km in favourable weather conditions and showed red to the west side and white to the east side of Broadhaven Bay and seaward.

On 1 December 1932, the Ballyglass lighthouse became un-manned while in 1977 the lights were converted to electric.

Like many lighthouses, the locality and the physical structures of the Ballyglass lighthouse provide some wonderful opportunities for photographers and sight-seers alike. Don't forget your camera on your next trip on the North Mayo section of the Wild Atlantic Way!

Clare Island lighthouse is another gem of a structure along the northern flank of Clare Island. The lighthouse was originally built by the Marquess of Sligo (of Westport House fame) in 1806. A careless lighthouse keeper attempted to dispose of the 'snuffings' of wick candles in 1813 but they caught fire and burned down the building. It was re-built and re-commissioned in 1818. It then operated continuously until September 1965 providing a flashing light every 5 seconds with a range of over 20 miles in good weather conditions.

Today, Clare Island Lighthouse is an iconic, though not in-expensive, guest house providing bed and breakfast plus dinner accommodation which is unique in Ireland. Just another tempting location to help your enjoyment of what beautiful Mayo has to offer...

Ballyglass lighthouse (Photo: F Sweeney)

Clare Island Lighthouse (Photo: Michael McLoughlin)

Clare Island Lighthouse (Photo: Michael McLoughlin)

IRELAND WEST AIRPORT KNOCK

Ireland West Airport (Photo: IWAK)

Ever since the first three Aer Lingus charter flights flew out of Knock Airport en route to Rome in October 1985, the airport has become one of the premier symbolic icons of County Mayo. Over thirty years later, the dreams of Monsignor James Horan, then Parish Priest of Knock, have more than delivered on his vision for a new, vibrant port of entry to the west of Ireland. Horan's ideas were ridiculed in many quarters – an Australian Sixty Minutes television crew sought to make fun of a rural priest seeking to build an airport in the middle of nowhere and on top of a mountain. History now tells us they got that attempt at ridicule very wrong indeed.

One of the great success stories in the building of the airport was that it was built on a shoestring budget with a small local construction company owned by Frank Harrington from Glantavraun appointed to develop the site and build the infrastructure. Less than E10 million in funding was provided from the Irish government with an additional E1.3 million from the European Union - but only on the proviso that there was matched funding from the developers.

In today's money terms, the construction costs of Knock Airport rank as the bargain of the century. In the process, Frank Harrington's company became an Irish icon proving much needed employment to the local hinterland. And he became a very wealthy man!

First flight Fr Horan (Photo: IWAK)

The first few years of the airport were not without its problems or its detractors. The location of the airport on the crest of a hill at an elevation of 203 metres in Kilgariff, some 5 kms south of Charlestown, posed problems especially in cloudy, foggy weather. Many flights in the early years had to be diverted to Shannon and the bussing of passengers between the two airports led many at the time to question the location of the airport and whether it would ever be a success.

But passengers from all over the west and north-west of the country loved using Knock Airport and its ideal location towards the middle of the country. Most of all, the travelling public loved its ease of access for arrivals and departures. By 1988, over 100,000 passengers were using the airport in a single year.

A huge bonus that guaranteed the success of the airport was extra developmental and infrastructural work undertaken in 2007-2009 with support from the Irish Government and the European Union. Most of the issues with poor visability in bad weather were relieved with the installation and implementation of Category 11 Instrument Landing System (CAT 11 ILS) on the main runway. The numbers of diversions due to bad weather dropped significantly and soon such events were no longer the focus of pub-talk and ridicule among the detractors.

The success of the airport changed the local landscape forever. Most aircraft approaching from the east fly over Mullaghanoe which is now populated with many navigational aids rather than local families out saving turf as in former years. Knock Airport is now on the flight path for thousands of international travellers but most of these are likely to be totally unaware of its history. Those with flight scanners can on any given day track flights from New York to Dubai, Frankfurt to Miami or Los Angeles to Rome, all with Knock Airport as a key reference point on their journeys.

Many of our predecessors in Mayo would shake their heads in disbelief if a development such as Knock Airport was foreshadowed some forty or fifty years ago. Back then, the twice daily passenger and occasional goods train on the Sligo to Claremorris railway line on the northern horizon provided the only serious distraction as well as obligatory time check for those enjoying a day on the bog.

Knock Airport is now officially known as Ireland West Airport Knock but its official IATA code – NOC -tells us exactly what it is. The airport continues to grow with over 800,000 passengers using the facility in 2018. The predicted 1 million passengers in a single year is not too far away.

The airport boasts a single main east-west runway of 2,300 metres with demonstrated capacity to handle large international jet aircraft including the Boeing 747 and Airbus A380. The number of regular scheduled and charter flight destinations continues to grow and currently is in the mid-20s. Ryanair has been a key partner in the development of the airport with flights to London Stansted and London Luton among the best supported.

International charter flights to New York and Boston have occurred while holiday and pilgrimage flights to European destinations are now more firmly established parts of the airport's business. In August 2018, Pope Francis flew into and out of Ireland West Airport as part of his historic visit to Knock Shrine during the second papal visit to Ireland.

It was a pity that Monsignor Horan did not survive long enough to be there to personally meet him. No doubt his statue along the airport approach road was pointed out to the Pontiff on his first visit to County Mayo. Monsignor Horan would have felt so very proud as to how well his vision for Knock, County Mayo and Ireland had turned into everyday reality.

RTE's Tommie Gorman interviews Fr. Horan at Knock Airport (Photo: IWAK)

Airline partners Aer Lingus Flybe and Ryanair (Photo: IWAK)

GREAT WESTERN GREENWAY

The **Great Western Greenway** which stretches from Westport through Newport and Mulranny and onto Achill Island has rapidly developed into one of County Mayo's premier tourist attractions. Roughly following the old railway line built in 1894 and operating up until 1937, the Greenway has become a tourist magnet with many families and individuals planning holiday breaks to walk and cycle the 26-mile (42 km) route along the panoramic Clew Bay coastline.

Mulranny Tide Out (Photo: Oliver Whyte)

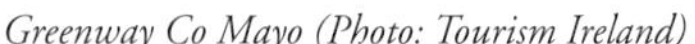

Greenway Co Mayo (Photo: Tourism Ireland)

Sheep dip Mulranny (Photo: Oliver Whyte)

The 18 km Newport to Mulranny section of the Great Western Greenway was the first to be constructed and opened in April 2010. Its tourism value was quickly appreciated with the section being awarded one of the European Destinations of Excellence awards for Ireland in 2011. Further construction followed with the Westport to Newport (11 km) and Mulranny to Achill Island (13 km) sections. The Greenway extension from Achill Sound to Saula opened in April 2018. The official opening of the Great Western Greenway on 29 July 2011 was by Islandeady-born Taoiseach (Prime Minister),

Minister Rings opens Achill Sound to Saula Greenway (Photo: MR)

Enda Kenny T.D. and Westport-born Minister of State for Tourism and Sport, Michael Ring T.D. Funding for the project came from both the Department of Transport, Tourism and Sport and Failte Ireland and cost E5 million with the development work undertaken by Mayo County Council. It too ranks as excellent value for money with domestic and international visitors showing their acknowledgement through their feet and pedal power.

The Greenway is entirely off-road and segregated from motorised traffic apart from a one-mile section through Newport. Visual highlights along the way include Westport House, panoramic views of Croagh Patrick and Clew Bay from numerous vantage points, the seven-arch railway viaduct in Newport, splendid mountain vistas of the Nephin Beg range between Newport and Mulranny, the coastal views around Mulranny itself as well as the mountains and coastal views on the section to Achill Island.

Apart from its great potential to attract tourism, another key plank in developing the mostly flat railway track was to encourage greater physical fitness and outdoor activities for all. Local hotels, bed and breakfasts and Air BnB along the route and in nearby towns and villages did not take long in recognising the potential offered by the increased tourist numbers to boost their businesses.

Old Railway Station, Mulranny (Photo: Oliver Whyte)

Mulranny Causeway Bridge (Photo: Oliver Whyte)

Goats lording it over Mulranny (Photo: Oliver Whyte)

The proximity of Ireland West Airport Knock has also stimulated this development with air travellers capable of travelling to Westport within an hour of arriving in the east Mayo airport. The numerous golf courses, fishing opportunities as well as mountain climbing in the county add variety to those with lots of energy to expend. The night life isn't bad either with numerous pubs, restaurants and hotels offering opportunities to quench a thirst or restore the glycogen levels and energy stores in tired muscles.

The success of the Great Western Greenway – the first in Ireland – has spawned similar developments in other areas throughout Ireland as well as a new development near Castlebar in Mayo itself. The new **Castlebar Greenway** stretches for 10 km from Lake Lannagh and follows a route mostly along the banks of the Castlebar River to The National Museum of Country Life in Turlough. The museum chronicles rural life in Ireland over the century from 1850 to 1950. The Greenway provides a mixture of farmland, wooded and river views along its route and is proving very popular with natives and tourists alike.

The Castlebar Greenway was officially opened by An Taoiseach, Enda Kenny T.D. and Minister of State for Transport, Tourism and Sport, Michael Ring T.D. on 1 May 2015. The development work was undertaken by Mayo County Council and involved 28 Permissive Access agreements with local landowners along the route. It is a welcome collaboration much appreciated by those availing of these excellent facilities. It is likely many more such developments will progressively emerge in other scenic parts of Mayo especially if pedestrian, cycling and accommodation facilities are well catered for.

Mulranny Park Hotel (Photo: Oliver Whyte)

Burrishoole reflections (Photo: Oliver Whyte)

Mulranny Causeway (Photo: Oliver Whyte)

Mulranny Village (Photo: Oliver Whyte)

THE CEIDE FIELDS

Ceide Fields Visitor Centre and Coastline (Photo: Marion Galt Ceide Fields)

Much of the credit for the exploration and development of the area of North Mayo now known as the Ceide Fields must go to archaeologist and Belderrig native, Professor Seamus Caulfield and his dad. Back in the 1930s, his school teacher father, Patrick Caulfield, noticed some peculiarities in the local bogs as he harvested his annual supply of turf. When he got down to the final spit of the bog, usually the source of the best quality, black turf (peat), he noticed some odd arrangements of stones that he could never fully understand and certainly never expected to encounter. Instead of stones or bog deal randomly strewn in the bog, he found neatly stacked heaps of stones that to his way of thinking just could not have happened by chance and they had to predate the laying down of blanket bog over the centuries and millennia.

Patrick Caulfield sought advice on his discovery through reporting it to the National Museum in Dublin. But crack-pot notions from the bogs of North Mayo were not given any high priority and the succeeding war years and a poor economy meant nothing happened till his son Seamus followed his own instincts and trained in archaeology and began exploring the same areas that intrigued his father. Using iron probes to pick out the pattern of the stone walls, what Seamus and his co-workers discovered was a system of well organised farming methods that immediately challenged the notion of a hunter-gatherer Mayo man of the distant past. Sophisticated carbon dating techniques were applied and these together with expertise from paleobotanists gradually put together a picture of farming more than 2,000 years old, some reckoning that it even pre-dated the Pyramids of Egypt.

Ceide Fields Old Pine (Photo: OPW, Ceide Fields)

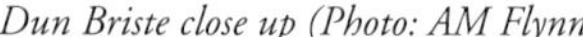

Dun Briste close up (Photo: AM Flynn)

Ceide Fields Cliff, (Photo: OPW, Ceide Fields)

The Ceide Fields lie close to Downpatrick Head in north County Mayo between Belmullet and Ballycastle. The site of the Stone Age and Bronze Age settlements form a unique part of our Mayo heritage. The Office of Public Works has constructed a pyramid-shaped interpretative centre at the site offering panoramic views as well as knowledge exchange on what the Ceide Fields stand for.

The development of the Ceide Fields represents an excellent example of the integration of high quality archaeological infrastructure linking the historical past with increasing public demand for better understanding of the lives and lifestyle of our predecessors.

It is well worth a visit on your travels along the north Mayo coastline and short day-tours are available for those who want to explore that little bit extra. A very old Scots Pine, some say up to 4,000 years old, occupies the centre of the Visitors Centre while the cliffs along the north Mayo coastline warrant a special visit for themselves.

Dun Briste framed (Photo: AM Flynn)

Sea Cliffs near Ceide Fields (Photo: MAYO.IE)

Ceide Fields night sky (Photo: Brian Wilson)

The Corrib Gas Field

When natural gas finally began to flow from the Corrib Gas Field off the north-west coast of Mayo on 30 December 2015, it marked the culmination of over 20 years of development that was often marked by its fair share of controversy. The original exploration licence to explore for oil and gas deposits in blocks of the seabed in an area known as the Slyne Trough Basin off the Mullet Peninsula was granted in 1993. In 1996 when the Corrib Natural Gas Field was discovered, it marked the first major, commercially-viable gas field in Ireland since the Kinsale Head Gas Field development that occurred back in 1971.

Fionnuala tunnel boring machine (Photo: Corrib Gas and Christy Loftus)

Initial plans for the development of the gas field met with dogged opposition from environmentalists and some locals with concerns about the safety of the proposed development. The main partners in the development phase of the project were Royal Dutch Shell (45%), the Norwegian Statoil group (36.5%) and Vermillion Energy Trust (18.5%). The plan involved developing a sub-sea production facility including half a dozen wells linked via individual flowlines to a central production manifold that in turn feeds the gas through a main pipeline to the onshore processing facility at the Bellanaboy Bridge Gas Terminal, near Belmullet.

The sheer size and logistics of the North Mayo development are enormous. The gas field itself is 52 miles off Erris Head and the sea in the area is 355 metres deep. The gas reservoir lies a further 3,000 metres under the seabed. The offshore laying of the gas pipeline involved welding together over 7,000 sections of 510mm (20 inch) diameter steel piping using the facilities of the Solitaire pipelaying vessel. Landfall for the 90 km pipeline is at Glengad. The onshore section involves a further 5 miles (9 km) of pipeline to the Bellanaboy Processing Plant where the natural gas is dried and any impurities removed. A feature of the Mayo field is that the mainly methane and ethane gas produced is of an exceptionally pure quality.

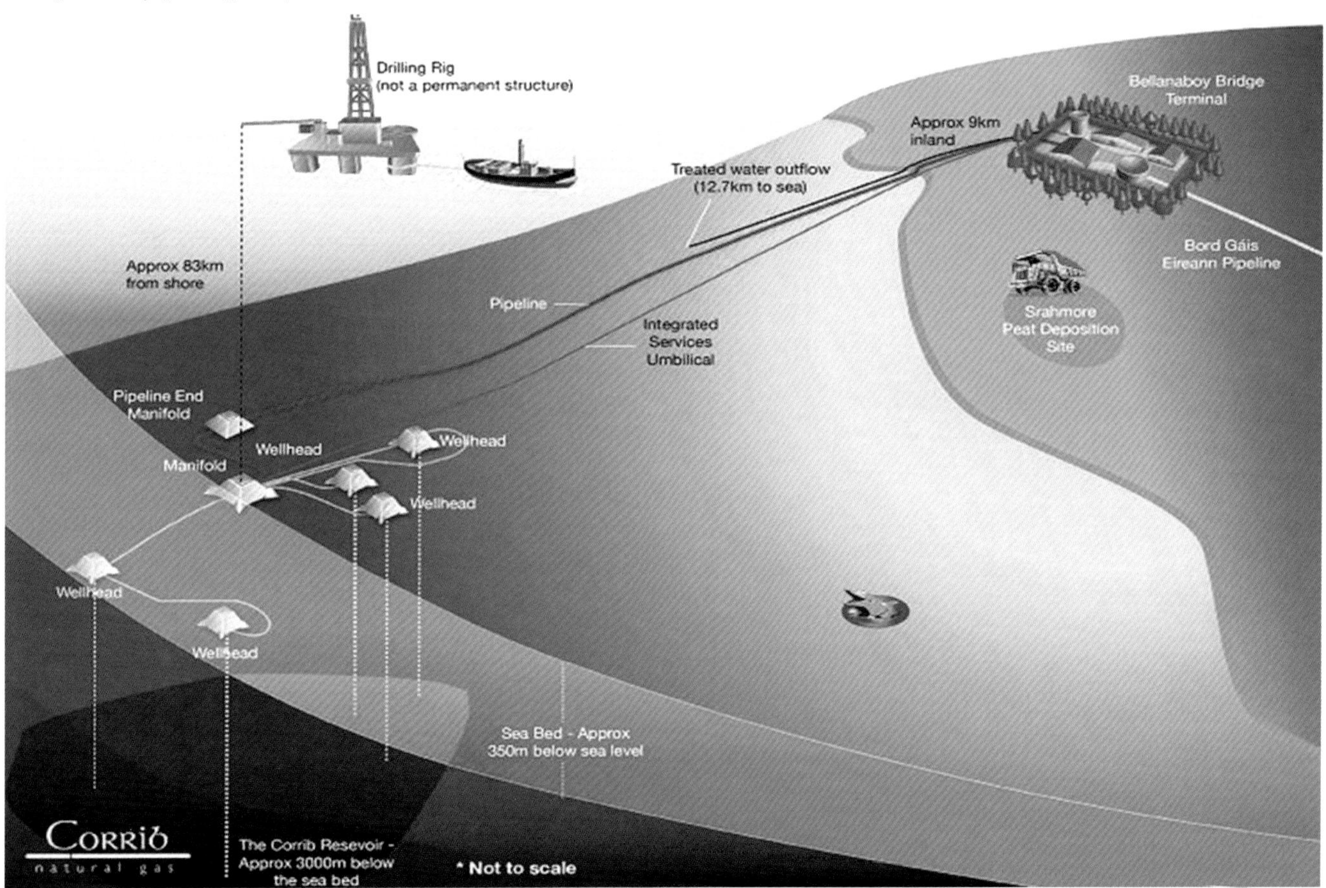

Schematic picture of Corrib Gas Field (Photo: Corrib Gas and Christy Loftus)

Natural gas that is processed from the Corrib Gas Field is fed into the Irish Bord Gais gas grid via the Gas Networks Ireland pipeline. It is estimated that the Mayo facility has the capacity to supply up to 60% of Ireland's gas requirements with an estimated 20 years life expectancy. The gas production is estimated to have the oil equivalent of up to 45,000 barrels a day. Shell estimated that up to 6,000 people worked directly or indirectly on the project over the years with over a billion Euros invested in Ireland.

In November 2018, Shell sold its 45% stake in the Corrib Gas Field Project to a Canadian Pension Plan Fund thus ending a 16-year association that had come with its fair share of controversy. Despite the lingering opposition in some quarters, Mayo's Corrib Gas Field project represents one of the largest developments in the county and continues to provide a contribution to Ireland's energy needs and helps support local employment and development.

The potential for further gas deposits in the seabed off the Mayo coast and close to the Corrib Field is being explored, adding the possibility of further significant contributions to our future energy needs.

Flaring Gas on Corrib Field (Photo: Corrib Gas and Christy Loftus)

Mayo Newspapers

Mayo has three major newspapers indigenous to the county – Western People, Connacht Telegraph and Mayo News while the Connacht Tribune from Galway city includes tracts of South Mayo in its readership. All were established in the latter part of the 20th century and have undergone significant transformations over the years.

Old Western People office Tone St, Ballina, 1962

The Western People

The Western People is a Ballina-based paper with offices in Castlebar. James Laffey is the current editor. It was established in 1883 by Patrick Grehan Smyth and T.A. Walsh and used the motto 'The West is Awake'. The paper's motto was changed in 1894 to 'The leading journal of the province'.

Ownership of the paper was for generations in the Devere family with a descendant Terry Reilly taking over the role of Managing Editor in the 1970s. Notable contributors over the years included stalwarts such as Jim McGuire, John

Healy (of Backbencher and Hurler on the Ditch fame), Michael Finlan and Liam Molloy. The dominance of the Western People was challenged for a while in 1977 with the start of the Western Journal which was one of the first regional papers to embrace the new printing technology including colour printing. The Western People was forced to follow suit to meet the challenge.

Connaught Telegraph Commemorative Issue 1996

Increasing costs, emerging technologies and off-site printing caused problems with financial viability of many regional newspapers. The ownership of the Western People eventually passed out of the Devere family to the Thomas Crosbie Holdings group, owners of the Irish Examiner. In more recent times with the demise of the Crosbie group, ownership passed to Landmark Media Investments before the paper was taken over by The Irish Times group in July 2018.

The Western used the traditional broadsheet format until 2013 when it changed to the current tabloid format. In 1979, publication day was switched to a Tuesday and was inspired by the visit of Pope John Paul 11 to Knock Shrine plus a smart realisation that dole day on a Tuesday meant some extra money in the pocket and luxuries such as the weekly newspaper could be justified. The move paid off handsomely as circulation numbers noticeably increased.

Like many regional newspapers, the Western has traditionally featured a large input of sporting events and commentary, both at the county level and locally, as well as extensive community news coverage and the paper's bread and butter, advertising. The paper's readership extends all over the county but still retains a solid heartland in the northern and eastern parts.

The Connaught Telegraph

The Connaught Telegraph (motto: Be just and fear not) was founded in 1829 by Lord Edward Cavendish though it was published as the Mayo Telegraph a year earlier in March 1828. Despite his personal title, Cavendish was a strong supporter of Home Rule for Ireland and was also supportive in attempts to improve the lot of the less well-off especially the lower classes in the county.

One of the most renowned and respected editors of the Telegraph was James Daly. In 1876, together with Alfred O'Hea, Daly became joint proprietor and editor. He continued as editor until 1892. After O'Hea's death in 1879, Daly was sole proprietor until 1880 when he sold it to employee and farmer, T.H.Gillespie.

Daly also had an active social and political life and combined with both Davitt and Parnell in many land reform activities. After the formation of the Land League in Daly's Hotel (the current Imperial Hotel) on the Mall in Castlebar in 1879, Daly was appointed its first secretary. He was involved with Michael Davitt in the large public Land League meeting at Irishtown in April 1879 as well as another event in Gurteen, County Sligo with Davitt after which they were both arrested and jailed only for the charges to be dropped at the subsequent trial. His anti-violence approach was enlightened and helped engender support against the excesses of the landlords.

In more recent times, the Connaught Telegraph struggled with increasing costs, new technology and wages growth. The paper, which at the time was owned by the Connolly family, went into voluntary liquidation in 2014 before being taken over by the Celtic Media Group. The paper is published every Tuesday and switched from the broadsheet to the compact format after its acquisition in 2014. The offices of the paper are in Castlebar with readership extending throughout the county. The paper focusses on news, sport and entertainment with a strong interest in local community events.

The Mayo News

The Mayo News which was founded in Westport by William and Patrick Dorriss in 1892 is currently edited by Michael Duffy. Like other regional newspapers, the Mayo News has a strong focus on local and community news, sport as well as entertainment.

The Mayo News has twice won significant industry awards – in 2007 and 2014 – as European Newspaper of the Year in the local newspapers' category. In the Local Ireland Media Awards in 2014, the paper was the winner in two areas – Best Designed Newspaper and Best Sports Story of the Year.

Back in the 1890s and 1900s, the paper highlighted the plight of tenant evictions, their cruel treatment by landlords and instances of police brutality in County Mayo. The early years of the paper coincided with the period after the Great Famine when the exploitation of Ireland by absentee landlords contributed in no small way to the destitution of many tenant families at the time.

In July 1897, the Mayo News reported with little fanfare on the death of Captain Charles Cunningham Boycott whose name has become synonymous worldwide on the withdrawal of support where foul deeds have been committed. Boycott's abuse of his tenants in his role as land agent for Lord Erne's estate (he lived in Lough Mask House on the shores of Lough Mask near Ballinrobe, County Mayo) empowered the local Land League activists to universally deny him the means of production on the estate and ostracised him both socially and financially.

The Mayo News recorded his passing as follows: 'The death of Captain Boycott, which took place last week at his residence, Flixton near Bungay, England attracted but little attention and was barely mentioned in the daily papers. Yet it is no exaggeration to say that his name will live forever.'

Sometimes saying very little can mean so much more. Within a decade the word 'boycott' had entered the lexicon worldwide and has remained there ever since.

The Mayo News

MIDWEST RADIO

MidWest Radio is Mayo's premier local radio station. The broadcasting studios are located on Clare St in Ballyhaunis and can be heard on FM at 96.1 KHz frequency. The station is owned by County Mayo Radio Ltd and long-term presenter of the Mid-Morning Show, Paul Claffey, is the station's Chief Executive Officer.

Apart from radio coverage across the entire county of Mayo, the station has a wide following across all Connacht counties plus some adjoining midland areas as well. Due to the world-wide web, MidWest also has a very wide international following via the Internet where it caters to the needs of the extensive Mayo diaspora. The international streaming is especially welcome in far off places at times of major sporting occasions especially if Mayo county or club teams are in action.

While MidWest is the default radio station for most Mayo homes and car travellers, it is not uncommon for Mayo exiles in Chicago, Fremantle or Vancouver to remain tuned in and hear some local news items like a stray calf on the road in Aghamore, an upcoming fund-raising event for a needy cause or the daily death notices.

MidWest Radio first hit the airwaves in July 1989 following a brief unlicenced period of broadcasting. For the past thirty years it has maintained a strong Country and Western flavour to its musical output though more modern recordings occasionally get a run. Tommy Marren has been a key personality with MidWest since the beginning and apart from his daily programme aptly named the Tommy Marren Show, doubles as the Station Manager. Gerry Glennon is another longstanding presenter and producer of radio programmes and in recent times has combined with Paul Claffey to produce Ireland West Music TV which is available on most week nights on Sky Channel, FreeSat or Freeview.

Paul Claffey (seated), Tommy Marren and Gerry Glennon (Photo: MWR)

The station boasts one of the highest listenerships in the country and operates from 7 am each day. Overnight MidWest reverts to an automated service with some replays of the most popular programs of the day and music.

If you are not a regular follower of MidWest Radio be sure to tune in to 96.1 MHz on your next visit to Mayo!

SECTION 3

HISTORY

Mayo Legion flag (Photo: Westport House)

ROMAN, VIKING, NORMAN AND MONASTIC INFLUENCES ON MAYO

Burrishoole Abbey (Photo: Tom Brett)

Killala Round Tower (Photo: MAYO.IE)

The Romans never invaded or tried to conquer Ireland but they were aware of our existence and referred to our island by its Latin name, Hibernia. The closest Roman contacts were probably through trading with Scotland and Wales and there is evidence such as coins and other artefacts supporting contact existed between the two islands.

Records tell us that from 795 AD Vikings from modern day Norway came in their long boats off the eastern coast of Ireland. Settlements tended to be mainly coastal especially in the period up to about 840 AD. There were no Viking settlements in Mayo but it is likely that raiding parties tried to plunder monasteries and other potential sources of wealth.

From 849 the raiding Vikings were mainly Danish and they were often engaged in fighting their Norse fellow invaders. Irish resistance ebbed and flowed with inter-marriage and assimilation of Irish ways another factor. At the Battle of Clontarf in 1014, the High King of Ireland Brian Boru defeated a large Viking army. Relative peace ensued over the next century apart from Irish chieftains from the four provinces often fighting for control of who would succeed to the title of High King.

Between the tenth and twelfth centuries many of Mayo's iconic round towers were constructed as part of monastic settlements. Apart from acting as places of sanctuary and look-outs, round towers also acted as bell-towers for the monks and the local people to call them to prayer and Mass and to provide safe storage for manuscripts, relics and other treasures. Mayo has five excellent examples of these structures at Turlough, Meelick, Killala, Balla and Aghagower.

After the death of Turlough O'Conner in 1156, his son Ruaidri succeeded him and later assumed the role as High King of Ireland. Diarmuid MacMorrough, King of Leinster, was under pressure to hold onto his realm and sought help from the Normans to help regain his kingdom which he had lost in 1166. The Norman invasion into Waterford Harbour in August 1169 radically changed the course of Irish history and had effects eventually in County Mayo. MacMorrough offered his daughter Aoife in marriage to Richard de Clare (Strongbow) and promised him succession as King of Leister after his death. The English Pope at the time, Adrian IV, gave his approval for the invasion of Ireland.

Ballintubber Abbey (Photo: Tom Brett)

Moyne Abbey (Photo: Tom Brett)

When Pope Adrian IV issued the Papal Bull 'Laudabiliter' he gave Henry II the permission of the Church to invade Ireland stipulating that it was 'for the correction of morals and the introduction of virtues, for the advancement of the Christian religion.' The Bull proved to be very controversial and it remains the most remembered part of that pope's historical legacy.

Over the next few years, the combined Norman invaders led by Henry 11 and Strongbow managed to secure the major towns of Wexford and Waterford as well as Dublin. Ruaidri O'Connor and Irish chieftains retaliated and attacked Dublin. The Treaty of Windsor acknowledged Henry 11 as overlord of the conquered lands and cities with Ruaidri O'Connor recognised as overlord of the remainder of the country. The Treaty only lasted a short time and the Norman acquisition of land and property continued apace.

The best agricultural lands were in the provinces of Munster and Leinster and these were targeted first. Connacht was less of a priority and with the overthrow of Ruaidri in 1186, the native Irish grip on power gradually waned. His brother Cathal Crobderg O'Connor became King of Connacht but with his death in 1224, one of the Norman invaders, Richard de Burgo, was granted most of the province of Connacht. Ruaidri O'Connor retired to Cong after being deposed and died there in 1198. The de Burgo link to Mayo continued while native Irish families such as the O'Connors progressively lost control. Close links between the de Burgos and the de Barris saw the latter establish themselves in Castlebar with their castle eventually lending its name to the town.

Monastic settlements continued to flourish in the Norman and Anglo-Norman eras. Because they were Christians, the Normans were not prone to plundering the treasures of the monasteries as happened in the Viking era.

The earliest monasteries in Mayo were at Ballintubber, Cong, Mayo Abbey and Errew. Ballintubber was founded by the Augustinians in 1216 and Mass has been celebrated continuously there ever since. The Franciscan friary at Sraide was built by Jordan D'Exeter in the 1240s and transferred to the Dominicans in 1252. Other Dominican abbeys founded during the 1400s included Urlaur Abbey near Kilmovee under the patronage of the Mac Costellos and Burrishoole under Richard de Burgo of the Lower MacWilliams.

The Carmelites established an abbey near Claremorris in the 1280s with support from the Prendergasts. The Augustinians established friaries at Ballinrobe in 1312 under the patronage of the de Burgos and later developed further houses at Ardnaree (early 1400s), Ballyhaunis (1430), and Murrisk (1456), the latter with support from the O'Malleys.

Across the Sligo border on the River Moy at Benada a further Augustinian abbey was built with support from the O'Haras in 1423.

Monasteries and friaries continued to prosper in Mayo and throughout Ireland in the period after the Second Lateran Council in 1215. Governance for new settlements was approved provided the religious orders adhered to church regulations. This relative peace and prosperity continued up until the reign of Henry VIII and the Reformation in the sixteenth century when the dissolution of the friaries and abbeys took place.

The Irish loss at the Battle of Kinsale was a turning point in the demise of the old Gaelic order while Cromwell's reign of terror between 1641 and 1653 saw any remaining resistance suppressed. The Cromwellian Settlements that followed meant Catholic lands were taken over and Irish landowners forced to move West of the Shannon including County Mayo.

Moyne Abbey (Photo: MAYO.IE)

Turlough Round Tower (Photo: Tom Brett)

Rosserk Friary (Photo: Tom Brett)

DE BURGO-O'MALLEY CHALICE

This silver gilt chalice is only 23cm high and is perhaps the finest example of a fifteenth-century chalice in Ireland. The octagonal stem has a knop with diamond shaped projections with blue and green enamel insets. Underneath the base of the chalice is a Latin inscription:

Thomas de Burgo et Grania Ni Malle me fieri fecerunt Anno Domini MCCCCLXXXXIIII.

Thomas de Burgo and Grania Ni Malle caused me to be made A.D. 1494.

Thomas de Burgo (Burke, who was also known as Crosach, meaning 'scarred'), who commissioned the chalice, was the grandson of Richard Bourke, the founder of Burrishoole Abbey, and it has been suggested that the chalice was made for the monks there. Thomas Burke's wife, Gráinne O'Malley, is probably a great-grandaunt of the more famous Gráinne (Grace) O'Malley, alias Granuaile.

Burrishoole chalice (Photo: Mayo.IE)

The Children of Lir

One of the great fables of Irish mythology has links to the small island of Inishglora off the Mullet peninsula in County Mayo.

Bodh Dearg and Lir, the legendary sea king, were great rivals and both wanted to be King of the Tuatha De Danann. Bodh Dearg was the victor but in an attempt at appeasement gave rival Lir his daughter Aoibh as a wife.

Aoibh and Lir subsequently had four children, a daughter Fionnuala as well as three sons, Aodh and twins Fiachra and Conn. Sadly, Aoibh died young. Bodh Dearg then offered Lir another of his daughters, Aoife, in her place and she became step-mother to the young children.

Children of Lir sculpture (Photo: Failte Ireland)

The first years were happy but then Aoife became very jealous of Lir's great love of his four children. Aoife considered having the children killed but instead opted to use her magical powers to have the four transformed into swans with a nine-hundred-year sentence to wander the lakes, rivers and seas of Ireland before eventually reverting to human form when the magical spell expired.

The first three hundred years saw them on Lough Derravaragh in County Westmeath followed by a similar length on the Sea of Moyle between the north-east coast of Ireland and Scotland with the final three hundred years on Sruwaddacon Bay, off Erris in County Mayo.

During the 900 years that the Children of Lir wandered around Ireland, the country was converted to Christianity. At the end of their time off Mayo, the swans flew to Inishglora island. On hearing the sound of a monk's bell, they suddenly reverted to human form. The local monk discovered their withered bodies and baptized them. The four died soon afterwards and were buried on Inishglora.

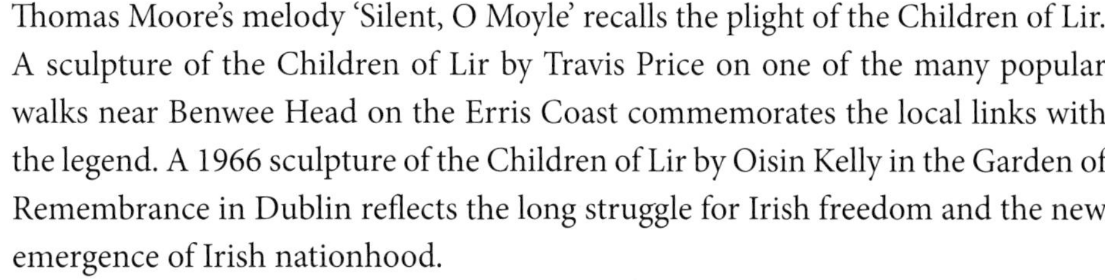

Thomas Moore's melody 'Silent, O Moyle' recalls the plight of the Children of Lir. A sculpture of the Children of Lir by Travis Price on one of the many popular walks near Benwee Head on the Erris Coast commemorates the local links with the legend. A 1966 sculpture of the Children of Lir by Oisin Kelly in the Garden of Remembrance in Dublin reflects the long struggle for Irish freedom and the new emergence of Irish nationhood.

Children of Lir Carrowteige (Photo: MAYO.IE)

Legend tells us the four children were all buried together, standing upright, in the one grave. Fionnuala was placed in the middle, Fiachra and Coon on either side with Aodh placed in front of her.

THE SPANISH ARMADA AND MAYO

Historical Perspective

It is difficult to appreciate the reasons why some of the ships and seamen of the Spanish Armada spent time in Mayo waters and on Mayo soil in the autumn of 1588 without some appreciation of the political and religious events occurring on the world stage at that time. Philip 11 was King of Spain and Elizabeth 1 was Queen of England back then and while England and Spain had been allies and on friendly terms in the early part of the 16th century, things took a turn for the worst in 1568 when Spanish forces occupied the Netherland/Flanders region, almost on England's doorstep.

Henry V111 had succeeded to the throne of England in 1509 at the age of 17 years. He married the Catholic, Catherine of Aragon that year. Their first surviving child was Henry, Duke of Cornwall, born in 1511 but he died after two months. A daughter, Mary, was born in 1516 and raised as a Catholic. She later married Philip 11 of Spain in 1554 but no children emerged from their union. She died in 1558. Catherine had four additional pregnancies but all were either stillborn or died shortly after birth.

Henry V111's second wife was Anne Boleyn and they produced a daughter, Elizabeth, who was born in 1533 and died in 1603. Elizabeth remained unmarried but had two pregnancies that ended in miscarriages. Anne Boleyn's marriage to Henry ended and she was beheaded in 1536.

Henry V111 also had a son, Edward, born in 1537 from his marriage to Jane Seymour. The Protestant Edward V1 succeeded his father as King in 1547 at the age of 9 years. His life was marred by poor health and he died seven years later in 1553 at the age of 16 years. He never married and had no children. On his death, his Catholic step-sister Mary succeeded to the throne. Her marriage to Philip 11 of Spain was not well received by the Parliament in Westminster

Blacksod Bay (Photo: MAYO.IE)

who reluctantly accepted him as Mary's consort but without any rights to eventually succeed her as King of England. On Mary's death, Elizabeth 1 became the first Protestant Queen of England in 1558. It was reported that Philip 11 had proposed marriage to Elizabeth but history tells us that offer was never accepted.

The invasion of the Spanish Netherlands by Spain in 1568 meant Philip now had a convenient launching pad for a potential invasion of England. Gradually Spanish forces gained control in the Netherlands prompting Elizabeth to offer military and financial support to her fellow Protestant Dutch resistance fighters. Elizabeth also used a strategy of attacking other Spanish sources of wealth and commerce including South America and the Caribbean. English sea-farers including Sir Francis Drake undertook raids on Spanish ships and territories to plunder some of their wealth.

Philip 11 countered with a proposal to develop an Armada of ships to sail up the English Channel to the Netherlands, rendezvous with their local commander there, the Duke of Parma, and proceed with plans to invade England. An ambitious raid by Drake in 1587 on the port of Cadiz resulted in the destruction of over 30 ships and large numbers of barrels being built to sustain the Armada. Their plans were delayed for a year and England got some breathing space to plan their defences.

When the 130 ship Spanish Armada with 30,000 men on board under the command of the Duke of Medina Sidonia sailed up the English Channel in July 1588, their crescent shaped formation made it difficult for the English naval forces to attack. The Armada reached Gravelines, near Calais, where they sought to consolidate before joining forces with their army in the Netherlands prior to an invasion of England.

70 metre waves over Eagle Rock Lighthouse (Photo: Anthony Hickey / Mayo.ME)

The English ploy was to attack the closely packed ships of the Armada using the burning skeletons of old ships loaded with combustible materials to drift into Spanish vessels made of timber and full of lethal amounts of gun-powder. Many of the Spanish ships had to cut their anchor lines to escape from a potential burning inferno and attempted to escape by sailing out to sea. The Armada had relied on four large galleons to protect their fleet but three were lost in the subsequent sea-battle. These losses seriously weakened their ability to attack or defend themselves.

The only option for the Spanish was to seek sanctuary via the North Sea as any possibility of a retreat down the English Channel towards home was now blocked off by the English. The more perilous route to the north of Scotland and down the west coast of Ireland meant the Spanish were now exposed to the vagaries of the North Atlantic and worsening September weather patterns. Their hope was that Catholic Ireland would offer some support for their salvation and a safe return to Spain. By late September 1588, the first retreating ships of the Spanish Armada were off the coast of Mayo.

Weather conditions off the north-west coast of Mayo in September 1588 offered no respite for the retreating and bedraggled Spanish Armada ships and their exhausted crews. Modern day meteorology tells us of massive ocean swells in the vicinity of key landmarks such as Eagle Rock off the Mullet peninsula on the approach to Blacksod Bay.

The Armada reaches Mayo

Of the reported 65 ships lost during the ill-fated Spanish Armada expedition, around 20 floundered off the Irish coast with about five of these occurring in Mayo waters. The best documented of these ships was La Rata Santa Maria Encoronada from the Squadron of Levant under the command Don Alonso Martinez de Leyna, a Spanish nobleman. His ship was an 820 ton carrack with a compliment of 419 men and 35 guns. As it retreated southwards in fierce storms off the Mayo coast on the 17 September 1588, it sought relief from the elements and an opportunity to replenish its dwindling food and water stocks and make some repairs, by entering Blacksod Bay. Unfortunately for Don Alonso and his crew, even the relative safety of Blacksod Bay did not prevent the ravages of the storm from impacting on his vessel. Because they had lost many of their key anchors in their determination to escape from English gunfire in the English Channel a few weeks earlier, their remaining anchors were insufficient to prevent them from running aground at Fahy Strand in Tullaghan Bay at the mouth of the Owenduff River, near Ballycroy on 21 September 1588. The crew all managed to make it safely onto Mayo soil bringing with them arms, guns, jewels and gold. They then secured Fahy Castle at Doona and burned their ship to prevent its potential future salvage by the English.

Don Alonso learned that two other Armada ships were anchored off Elly Bay to the seaward side of the Mullet peninsula. The Nuestra Senora de Begona (750 tons with 297 men and 24 guns) and the Duguesa Santa Ana (900 tons with 357 men and 23 guns). The survivors sought refuge aboard the Duguesa Santa Ana and headed north to Donegal where it floundered. Survivors then transferred to another Spanish ship, the Girona, which had been moored in Killybegs with rudder damage. A decision was made to head for safety in Scotland but the Girona was wrecked on rocks off Lacada Point near Giants Causeway in County Antrim. It has been estimated that of the 1,300 men on board the Girona, only nine survived. Some of the jewellery from the ship was recovered and is currently on show in the Ulster Museum. The Nuestra Senora de Begona meanwhile headed south to Spain which it reached in safety.

Other Spanish Armada ships lost off the Mayo coast are less well documented. These include El Gran Grin (336 men), San Nicolas (294 men), Ciervo Volanta (171 men and the Santiago (65 men). No exact records exist of other ships and it is possible that other sailors came onto Mayo soil but their fate remains unknown. The Governor of Connacht, Sir Richard Bingham, was less than sympathetic to the cause of the Spaniards and any survivors who were captured were likely to have been executed.

Of the total Spanish Armada fleet of 130 ships that departed Spain, only half (65 boats) managed to make it back to the safety of their homeland. How many had their lives spared through native Irish sympathisers remains unknown but it is possible that some Spanish genes are reflected in the olive skins of a few Mayo folk.

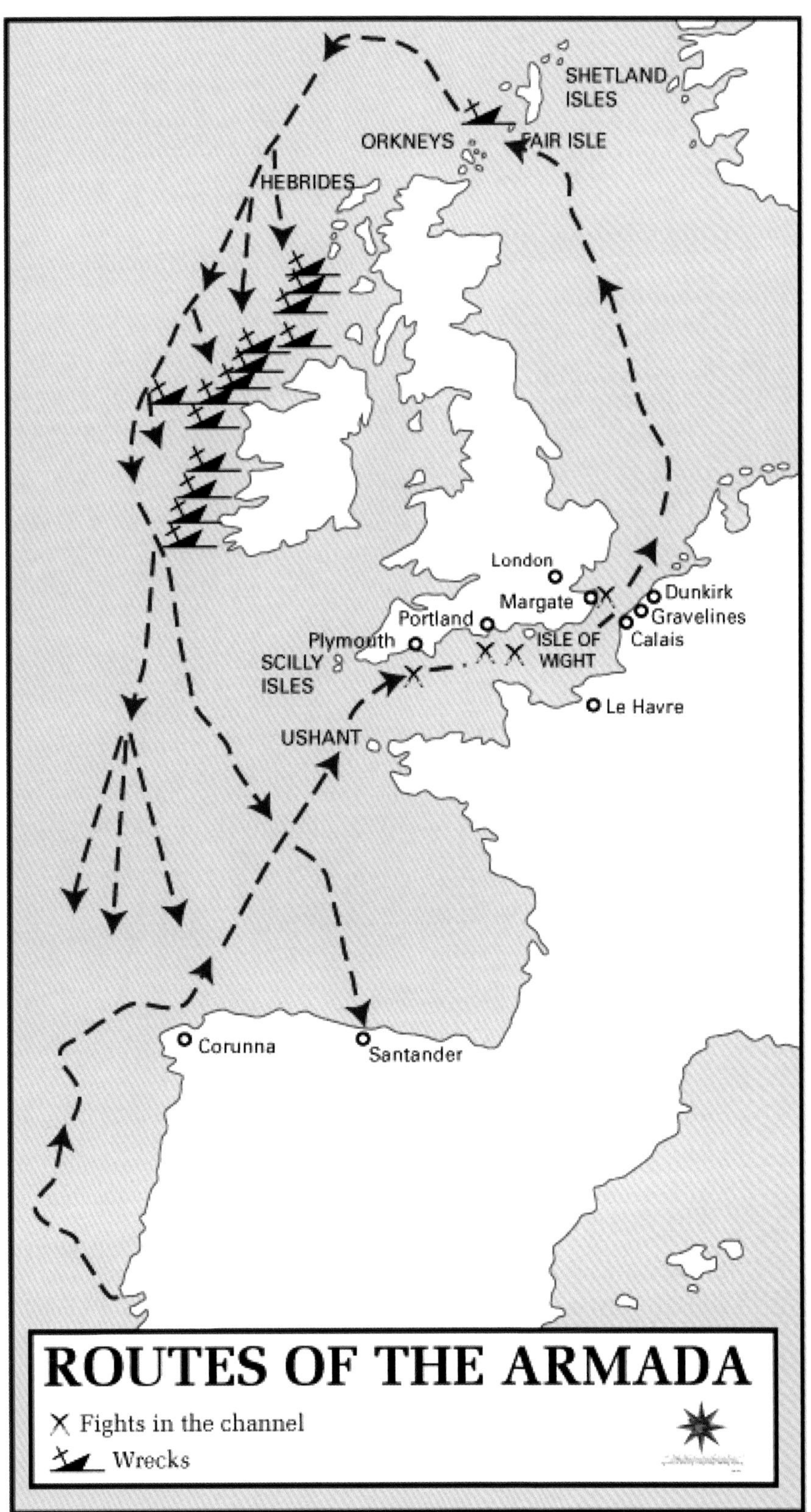

Spanish Armada Route 1588 - map drawn by History Dept of the United States Military Academy at Westpoint (Photo: Wikimedia Commons)

Big Houses

Westport House

Westport House is one of the premier big houses in Ireland currently open to the public. The original house was built by descendants of a Jacobite supporter, Colonel John Browne (1638 – 1711), whose family moved to Ireland from Sussex in England in the sixteenth century. Their land possessions initially were in The Neale area of County Mayo and their acquisition occurred in part through strategic marriages with native Irish landowners. Although the family at the time was Roman Catholic, the fact that their lands were in Connacht and thus far away from Cromwell's marauding armies, meant that the diktat of the English Republican – 'To Hell or to Connacht' – allowed the Browne family to hold onto their properties – at least for a while.

Browne's Mayo links began with his marriage to The Honorable Maud Bourke, daughter of the 3rd Viscount Mayo. She in turn was a great, great, granddaughter of Grainne Uaile (Grainne O'Malley), the legendary pirate queen of sixteenth century west of Ireland. The Browne – O'Malley alliance saw the family increase their estates in Galway and Mayo including Cathair na Mart (Fort of the Beeves) - an old, derelict O'Malley castle on Clew Bay.

Westport House

With the advent of the Williamite wars, the Browne family's fortunes plummeted. Defeats at the Battle of Aughrim in County Galway in 1691 and the failure of the Siege of Limerick later that year led to mass confiscations of their estates and serious decline in their fortunes. A small amount of property around Cathair na Mart was all that remained at the time of the Colonel's death in 1711.

He was succeeded by his son, John Browne IV who opted to change his religion to the Church of Ireland and attempted to consolidate his remaining lands and began some of the initial works on the development of Westport House. A keen farmer, his main legacy to the area was his plan for a new town in Westport and the establishment of a viable linen industry.

The first architect for the current Westport House was Richard Cassels and he was hired by John Browne IV to undertake the work in 1730. The first part of the house to be constructed was the eastern section and it faced directly onto the town. Richard Cassels was a German architect with many notable constructions in Ireland including Leinster House (current home of Dail Eireann), Russborough House in County Wicklow and Carton House in County Kildare. John Browne IV was rewarded for his endeavours by being made 1st Earl of Altamont in 1771. Successors to the title were his son Peter, 2nd Earl of Altamont, and grandson John Denis, 3rd Earl of Altamont.

The 3rd Earl was responsible for the establishment of the lake on the seaward side of Westport House, the building of the town of Louisburgh and a theatre located at the Octagon. He was also instrumental in securing the services of James Wyatt to construct facades on the north, south (dated 1778) and west of the house to form an enclosed quadrangle.

Wyatt was a famous English architect and some of the main architectural features of Westport House reflect his work. Wyatt's son, Benjamin, was responsible for the north and south wings. Further additions included a grand staircase, a library and a large dining room featuring mahogany doors imported from Jamaica where other family members owned estates some of which were linked to the slave trade.

The 1798 Rebellion of the United Irishmen, the arrival of General Humbert, the Races of Castlebar and the brief Connacht Republic under President John Moore of Moore Hall, all occurred during this time. General Humbert's troops briefly occupied Westport House after their Castlebar triumph.

The 3rd Earl's younger brother and MP Denis Browne took a more vicious approach to the insurgents as the rebellion failed and was responsible for ordering the hanging of many of its leaders. His reputation as the family's black sheep was not without strong evidence. John Denis Browne was created the 1st Marquess of Sligo after the Act of Union in 1800 but he only attended Parliament at Westminster on a few occasions.

Howe Peter - Lord Sligo

He was succeeded as 2nd Marquess of Sligo by his son Howe Peter Browne in 1809 at the age of twenty-one. His education at Eton and later at Cambridge brought him into contact with many of the political and literary luminaries of the day including a close friendship with Lord Byron. The new Marquess liked the good life and travelled widely including an infamous trip to Greece where he took possession of damaged green marble columns near Agamemnon's tomb at the Treasury of Atreus. In his zeal to get his treasures home to Westport, he press-ganged the services of some members of a British warship, an act that was frowned upon in London and subsequently cost him four month's jail-time at Newgate Prison.

Howe Peter subsequently married Lady Hester de Burgh, daughter of the Earl of Clanrickarde. He was now ready for family life in Westport and fourteen children (six sons and eight daughters) emerged from their union. Apart from his efforts at enhancing Westport House, his other passions were horse racing and Irish wolfhounds. After the 1811 flat racing season, Howe Peter bought the 1809 Epsom Derby winner, Pope, whom he later re-named Waxy Pope for his subsequent career as a breeding stallion.

In 1834 Howe Peter's career trajectory switched to Jamaica where he was appointed Governor (1834 – 1836) prior to the ending of the slave trade in the region. His family connections (the Kellys) owned slave plantations in Jamaica but towards the end of his stint as Governor Howe Peter played a part in slave emancipation with the first free village for ex-slaves named Sligoville in his honour.

Back in Ireland, Howe Peter Browne supported the introduction of Catholic Emancipation and was made Lord Lieutenant of Mayo in 1831. His corpulent figure graced the Houses of Parliament in Westminster for many years prior to his death in 1845 just as the Great Famine began to take its lethal grip on Ireland. Lord Lucan succeeded him as Lord Lieutenant of Mayo in 1845.

Octagon, Westport (Photo: Failte Ireland / Mayo.IE)

During the famine Westport House was closed but the Browne family were well regarded for their efforts to mitigate the effects of the great hunger on their starving tenants. George, the 3rd Marquess of Sligo, used his own funds to import meal through Westport Quay and helped the destitute at the workhouse in Westport. His efforts to encourage a more humane approach from London fell on deaf ears.

George was succeeded by his brother, John as 4th Marquess of Sligo in 1868 and like earlier family members before him, the job of rationalising and stabilising the family estate fell to him. Agrarian reform was now high on the political agenda with democratic ideals also starting to take hold. John put the agricultural basis of the estate on a firm footing while his successors including the 6th Earl added other features including a salmon fishery, tree plantations and an Italianate garden on the western side. In 1960, Denis, the 10th Marquess of Sligo and his son Jeremy, 11th Marquess decided to open Westport House and its gardens to the public.

For nearly 300 years until 17 January 2017, there was a direct Browne family connection with Westport House until its sale to the Hughes family who also hail from Westport. Hopefully, this unique feature of Irish history in the West of Mayo will continue to be available to many future generations.

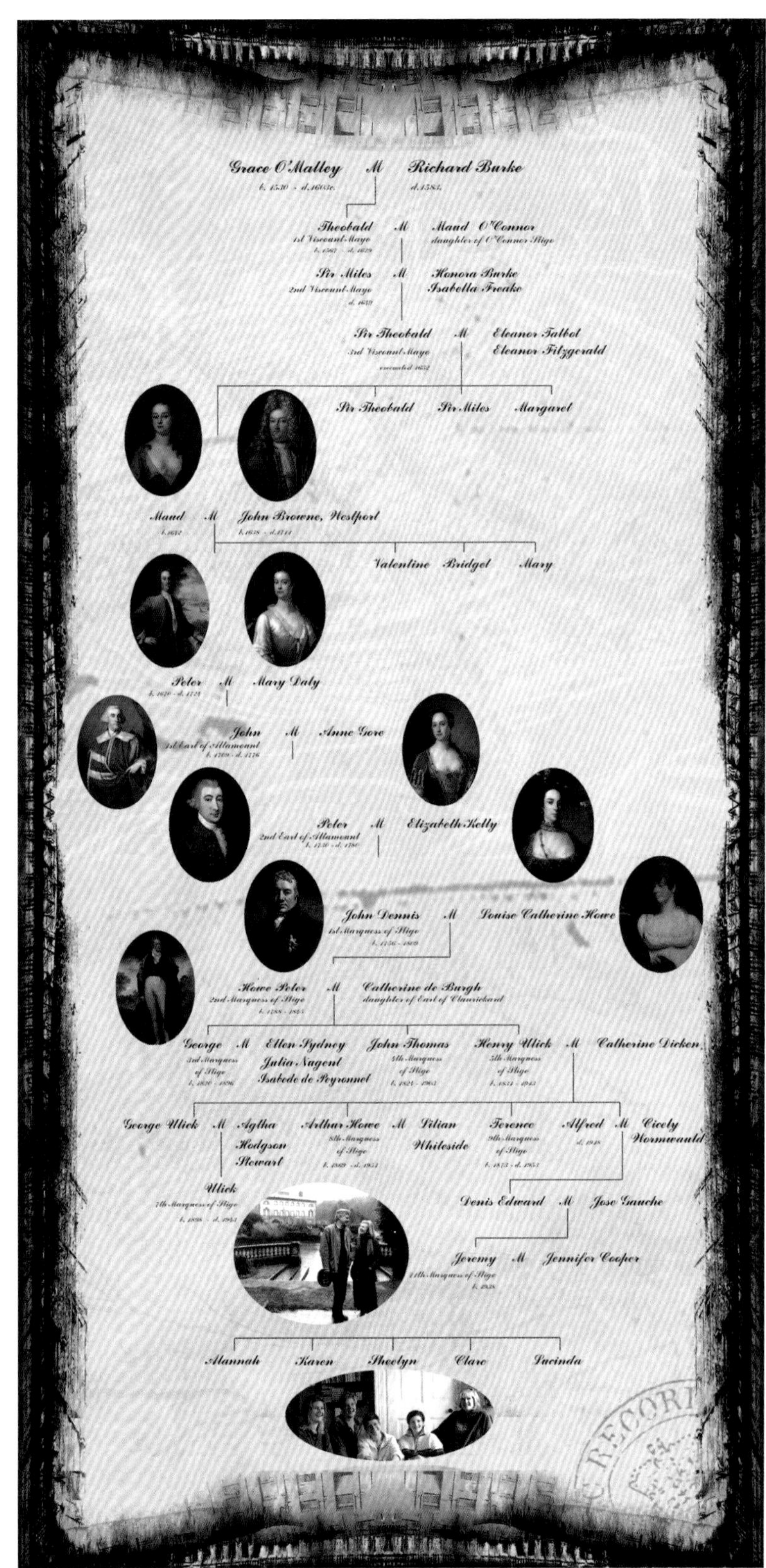

Westport House Family Pedigree (Photo: Westport House)

Moore Hall, near the village of Carnacon, is on the shores of Lough Carra. It has an interesting history starting with the fortune to build it that was acquired by its first owner, George Moore (1727 – 1799). As a younger man, George moved to the Alicante area of Spain where he became a leading trader in wine with extensive shipping interests. After selling his wine interests in Spain, George returned to Mayo and acquired a large picturesque site near Lough Carra. Moore Hall was built in the period between 1792 and 1796. The Big House was unusual at the time, rather like Westport House, in that its owners were of Catholic stock and George Moore was acknowledged for his more enlightened, humanitarian approach as a supporter of tenants' rights.

Shortly after construction began on Moore Hall, the rumblings of the United Irishmen and their quest for greater autonomy from England became more intense. The arrival of General Humbert and his French army in August 1798 caused political instability in County Mayo. George Moore's 32-year-old son John, then a law student in Dublin, was drawn by the ambitions of the Irish – French alliance in his home county.

After the rapid success of General Humbert at the Races of Castlebar, a Provisional Republic of Connacht was declared with John Moore as its first President. Unfortunately, victory was short-lived. General Humbert and his men were defeated at the Battle of Ballinamuck in County Longford after a few weeks. John Moore was arrested and thrown into prison. His father George tried to intercede on his behalf but while he was spared the hanging suffered by many of his countrymen, John was sentenced instead to deportation. He died in prison in Waterford the following year. His father George also died in 1799.

The Moore family produced some famous writers including George Augustus Moore. Most of the Moore Hall estate was sold to the Congested Districts Board in 1912 as part of agrarian reform at the time.

Walled Garden Moore Hall (Photo: Tom Brett)

Moore Hall (Photo: Tom Brett)

Moore Memorial Kiltoom (Photo: Tom Brett)

Moore Hall Driveway (Photo: Tom Brett)

During the Civil War after Irish independence from England, Moore Hall was burned to the ground on 1 February 1923 by anti-treaty forces. The building has remained derelict ever since. The lands around the house were subsequently developed as a forestry plantation by Coillte.

The house and about 80 acres of land around it were bought by Mayo County Council in 2018. The hope is that Mayo County Council will continue with its imaginative policy of developing historic sites such as the very successful Great Western Greenway between Westport and Achill. The restoration of Moore Hall to its former glory would be warmly welcomed in the area and in County Mayo.

Towerhill House, located on the western side of Lough Mask in the shadow of Partry mountains was built by the Blake family of Galway Tribes fame towards the end of the 18th century. One of the family's claims to fame was that it helped sponsor the first ever gaelic football match in County Mayo, a marathon two-hour affair. Of note, the team colours used by Carnacon, one of the competing teams, were green and red and these colours were subsequently adopted by Mayo for the county team. Young Irelander, Thomas Davis refers to the 'green above the red' in one of his celebrated poems.

Turlough Park House (Photo: Tom Brett)

Ownership of Towerhill House slipped from the Blake family with the death of batchelor, Valentine Blake, at the age of 81 years in 1947. The estate and house were sold to local landowners after his death. To save costs on paying rates on the house, the new owners removed the roof and all the valuables from the house which subsequently went into decay. A sad ending to a local landmark.

Other notable big houses in County Mayo include Barley Hill House Bohola, Clogher House, Newport House and Turlough Park House (built by the Fitzgerald family in 1865 and located close to the newly established Museum of Country Life in Turlough).

Museum of Country Life (Photo: Tom Brett)

War and the Year of the French

For a period of about a month over two hundred years ago in August-September 1798, Mayo held centre stage in an uprising against English rule in Ireland. Set in its historical context, the 1798 Rebellion in Ireland took place in the wake of two major world revolutions – the American Revolutionary Wars 1775-1783 and the French Revolution 1789-1799.

The Society of United Irishmen had been formed in Belfast in 1791 and had as one of its leaders a Dublin protestant lawyer, Theobald Wolfe Tone. The ideals of the American and French Revolutions involved equality and liberty and spearheaded a movement towards the birth of democracy. What started with the storming of the Bastille on 14 July 1789 eventually culminated with the demise of the era of absolute monarchies.

Initial uprisings of the United Irishmen in Leinster and Ulster were savagely put down by the ruling English military. But Irish soldiers had fought in France during the revolution there and the liberating ideals progressively filtered back home. Tone had also visited France seeking support to encourage sympathetic French powers to bring their revolutionary ideas back to Ireland.

In 1796, a large contingent of French soldiers set sail for Ireland with the aim of supporting the Irish and distracting the English from their wars with France. About 12,000 French soldiers arrived in Bantry Bay in December but because of severe storms and a failure of the entire party to meet at the designated landing area, the fleet decided not to try landing and instead retreated home to France.

On the 22 August 1798, a much smaller contingent of 1,060 soldiers on three galleons under the command of General Humbert landed on Kilcummin strand in Killala Bay in County Mayo. The French had arrived with Matthew Tone, a brother of Theobald, among them. Also included in the group was a Catholic priest with Killala connections, Fr Henry O'Kane and Bartholomew Teeling, an aide to General Humbert.

The French brought three cannons with them and about five thousand muskets. They quickly joined forces with about a thousand Irish supporters and overran limited English resistance in Killala. Their initial headquarters were in the grounds of the residence of the Church of Ireland Bishop of Killala, Bishop Stock. Word of Humbert's arrival soon spread and he moved quickly to secure the nearest English garrison at Ballina two days later. Local support involved marking the best approach to Ballina with lighted straw bundles, an event that led to the subsequent naming of Bothernasup (the road of straw) area in Ballina.

After Ballina, the next important objective was to secure the major garrison town of Castlebar. Along the way, further Irish support of up to 3,000 foot-soldiers joined the ranks but many were poorly armed with just pikes and pitchforks. The initial plan was to travel to Castlebar via Foxford but on the advice of Fr James Conroy of Lahardane, an alternate, much rougher route to the north and west of Lough Conn through Lahardane, Barnageeha and Bofeenaun was followed. The night trek was seriously curtailed by very inclement weather and lead to a decision to discard much of their heavy artillery. On the journey, the French soldiers and their Irish support were fed by local farmers and supporters.

The first engagement with the English was at Sion Hill outside Castlebar. General Humbert outflanked the English defenders under General Lake who then retreated with his soldiers down Staball Hill and attempted to defend the bridge on Main street. The outcome resulted in the English recognising their position as hopeless and instead of fighting they turned on their heels and retreated as quickly as they could towards Tuam and Athlone. Their ignominious defeat has passed into folklore as the 'Races of Castlebar' due to the speed of the retreating English forces.

Shortly after the capture of Castlebar, the towns of Westport and Newport were quickly secured. General Humbert's first headquarters in Castlebar was at Geevy's Hotel, now known as the Humbert Inn. A Provisional Government of Connacht was quickly declared by the victors with a sympathetic law student, John Moore of Moore Hall, installed as its first President.

Despite the initial successes, Humbert did not feel safe in Castlebar as an expected backlash from the English under Lord Cornwallis (of American Revolutionary Wars infamy) was to be expected. On 3 September 1798, Humbert and his army suddenly departed Castlebar heading towards Sligo on hearing the re-grouped English forces were within a day's march. Their route took them through Bohola, Swinford, Bellaghy (no Charlestown established back then!), Tubbercurry and onto Collooney.

The group covered a remarkable 58 miles in 36 hours but were soon under pressure from the English and had to hastily retreat to Ballyshannon and onto Dromahair in Leitrim. The final showdown occurred at Ballinamuck, County Longford on 8 September 1798. Lord Cornwallis's troops and those of General Lake used their superior numbers to surround Humbert's men and after 30 minutes of battle the French surrendered. The French were treated as prisoners of war but upwards of 2,000 Irish were massacred or hanged shortly afterwards. The main uprising had lasted 17 days and only a few remote areas offered any further resistance.

The last major encounter was the Battle of Killala on 23 September 1798. Reprisals became the order of the day for the Irish insurgents. John Moore was tried and convicted and sentenced to transportation. He died in prison in County Waterford while awaiting his fate. He was buried in Ballygunner Cemetery in Waterford but in 1961 his body was exhumed and re-interred on The Mall in Castlebar.

Catholic priests who supported the Rebellion were shown no mercy either. Fr Andrew Conroy of Addergoole and Fr Manus Sweeney of Newport were hanged for their involvement. Others to meet a similar fate included Colonel O'Dowd from Bonniconlon, Captain O'Malley from Burrishoole, and General Blake. Native-born Irish in the French Army such as Bartholomew Teeling, an aide to General Humbert, and Matthew Tone, were not spared either.

The 1798 Rebellion might have been short and ultimately failed in its primary objective but it was remarkable in that it was a non-sectarian revolt with both Protestant and Catholic fighting on the same side for ideals of equality and liberty that were gradually taking hold in many parts of the world. The English reaction was to pass the Act of Union without any Irish consent. But a new awakening had occurred and the privileged classes who sought to rule with an iron fist rather than consent soon realised those days were finally coming an end.

Bust of General Humbert (Photo: MAYO.IE)

Mayo Legion flag (Photo: Tom Brett)

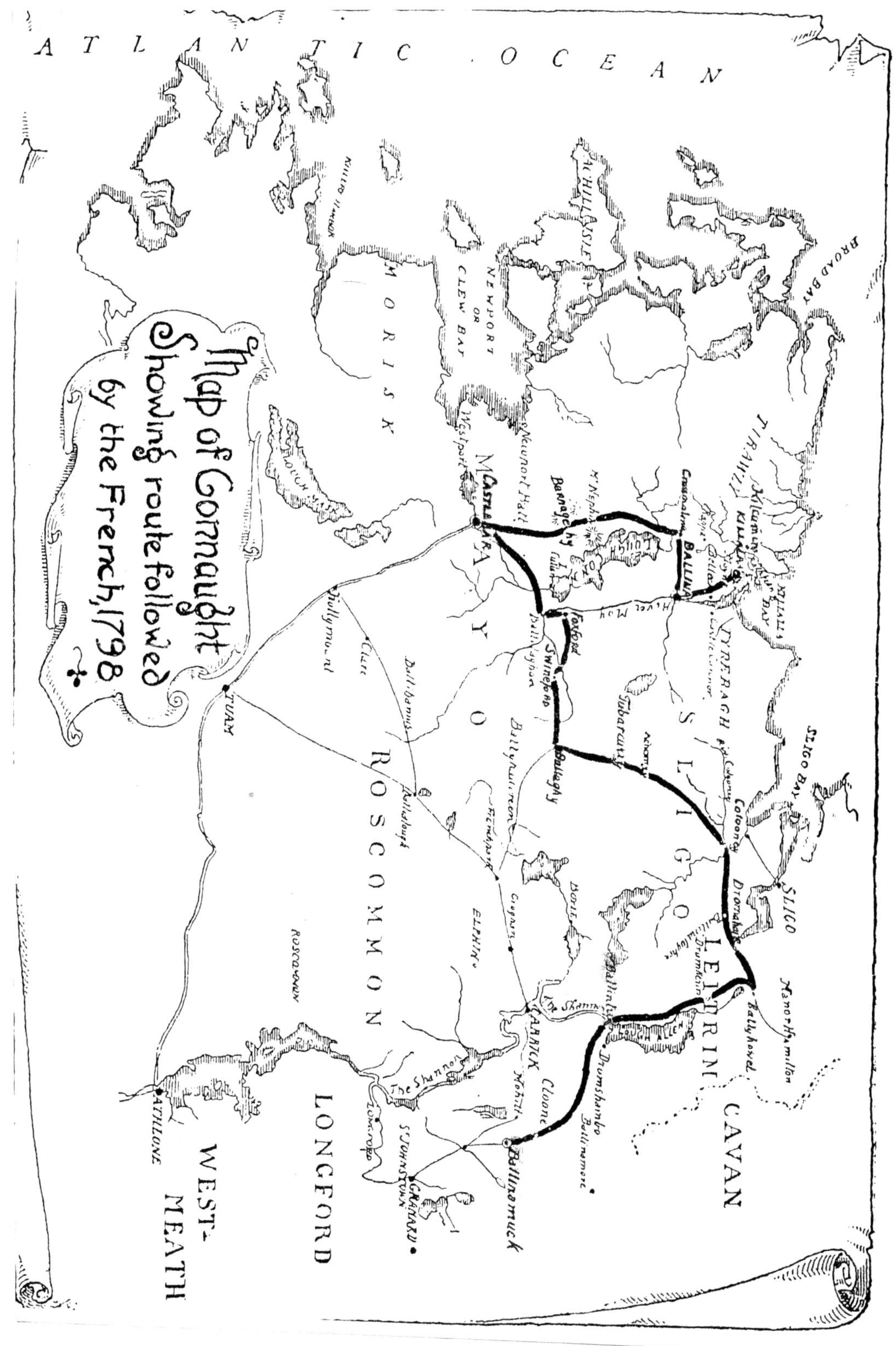

Map of French route in 1798 (Photo: Mayo Co Library Collection)

Famine and the Road to Delphi

For visitors to County Mayo, the Delphi area to the south-west confronts the traveller with examples of exquisite beauty on the one hand but a tragic, haunting past on the other. In parts of Mayo, contrasting the splendour of the region's geography with its equally excruciating history can sometimes be a challenging and uncomfortable experience.

The landscape and seascape between Westport and Louisburgh, especially around Murrisk in the shadow of Croagh Patrick, presents one of the most iconic panoramas of County Mayo. To the right lies Clew Bay with its numerous islands with Clare Island rising in majestic splendour further out to sea. Beyond Louisburgh as you head towards Leenane, the mighty Mweelrea (in Irish 'the bald king') mountain towers to the right with the equally impressive Sheffrey Hills on the left. In between the two lies the Doolough (the 'black lake') Pass and its various memorials to much bleaker times.

At the end of Doolough Lake, the mountain pass between the Sheffrey Hills and Ben Creggan offers a delightful opportunity for sightseeing on a lovely wilderness area. The pass forms part of the Mayo Way and while rather narrow with numerous hairpin bends, such discomforts are more than compensated by some very exciting and unforgettable scenery. Thankfully, traffic on the road is generally light and apart from the odd car, the only other inhabitants on the higher uplands are likely to be walkers, bikers and lots of mountain sheep grazing on the long acre.

Beyond Doolough Lake, you arrive at Delphi where the lodge, built by the Second Marquess of Sligo - who had visited Delphi in Greece – was then a playground of the gentry and the establishment. Today it is an adventure playground for walkers, fishers or those using its unique location as a base to soak up the area's history and geography. Further on, the road passes in to County Galway and Leenane village with its access to trips on the historic Killary Fjord – Ireland's own true fjord stretching for 12 km out westwards to the Atlantic Ocean.

But the real purpose of today's trip should be to learn a lot more of the events that happened along this historic road to Delphi in the mid-1800s – events forever etched into the folklore of this beautiful area of south-west Mayo. On a fine Summer's day, there are few more beautiful trips than a journey through Doolough Pass and onto Delphi. But on a cold, wet and wintery day the Pass is the complete opposite – cold, bleak and foreboding. Your aim should be to retrace the tragic footsteps of the 600 starving locals who during Ireland's Great Famine (An Gorta Mor) attempted to walk the 12 miles from Louisburgh to Delphi in search of a promise of food relief to quell their great hunger.

The date was 30 March 1849 and two officials of the Westport Poor Law Union, a Colonel Hogrove and Captain Primrose, were scheduled to inspect the starving men, women and children of the area who were seeking continuation of food relief. These local people had already endured five years of famine and there was no respite in sight. They were the poorest of the poor and qualified for support as they had less than a quarter of an acre of land. The meeting was scheduled for Louisburgh but when the starving people turned up there, they were told that Hogrove and Primrose had gone to Delphi instead and if they wanted to present for poor relief they should do so in Delphi by 7am the following morning.

Accounts vary but some 400-600 starving men, women and children trudged their way to Delphi that night in freezing, cold and wet conditions. Many never made it to Delphi and succumbed on the way. For those who survived the overnight walk to Delphi, they were told on arrival that the Poor Law officers were at lunch and could not meet them. Eventually, when they did meet no relief was offered to the starving wretches. Many of those who attempted the return journey to Louisburgh died on the way, some reportedly with grass in their mouths as they sought some sustenance to ward off their hunger.

Today, a Famine Walk celebrates the lives of those unfortunate people who died on the road to Delphi in 1849. The Doolough Tragedy 1849 memorial was erected to celebrate the memory of those who died in the Famine of 1845-49. Another memorial has the words of Mahatma Gandhi inscribed: 'How can men feel themselves honoured by the humiliation of their fellow human beings?'

It is hard to stop at the site of the Doolough tragedy and not feel the weight of its history hanging out from the nearby mountains or to visualise the reflections on the Black Lake of the ghostly walkers who made that fateful trek to Delphi back in 1849.

World leaders, clergy and many famous people have been similarly touched as they too walked the Road to Delphi. Archbishop Desmond Tutu, Kim Phuc – Vietnam's victim of a napalm bombing raid, the radiated children of Chernobyl and Sarajevo's Vedran Smailovic, have all felt drawn to similarly express their respect. Even the Choctaw Native American Indians in far-off Oklahoma recognised the significance of the place and the events that occurred in County Mayo. Their forebears sent a donation of $710 to Irish famine relief on hearing of the 1849 tragedy because it struck a chord with them and their own evictions from their native lands a generation earlier.

Your visit to Doolough Pass on the Road to Delphi will long remain in your memory from this historic journey through County Mayo. The circumstances of their deaths should be a clarion call for all of us in helping to minimise greed and man's inhumanity to man.

Doolough valley (Photo: MAYO.IE)

Famine ship Murrisk (Photo: MAYO.IE)

Doolough Pass Memorial (Photo: Tom Brett)

Michael Davitt and the Land League

Michael Davitt mid 30s (Photo: Mayo.ie)

Born in Straide, County Mayo on 25 March 1846 during the early years of The Great Famine, Michael Davitt soon learned at first hand the poverty and precarious living conditions endured by families of tenant farmers in Mayo at the time. Because of crop failures and the lack of alternative food to the then staple diet of potatoes, many families soon fell into rent arrears with the inevitable spectre of eviction a stark reality.

At the age of four years, Michael Davitt's family were evicted from their humble abode. The family eventually took the emigrant route and he ended up with his parents and three sisters in Haslingden in Lancashire. At the age of nine years Michael began work in the local cotton factory. Within two years disaster struck when he lost his right arm in a machine accident at work. His physical work capacity was limited as a result but, undaunted, Michael continued his education at a local Protestant school.

His interest in social and political reform and Irish history saw him join the Irish Republican Brotherhood and the Fenian movement in 1865 where he soon became organising secretary for England and Scotland. In 1871, he was arrested and sent to prison for smuggling arms to Ireland. On his release after seven and a half years, he maintained his interest in social reform especially attempts to modify the power of absentee landlords in Ireland and the poverty their absolute power inflicted on the tenant class. He founded the Land League in 1879 which was dedicated to the relief of the poverty of tenant farmers by seeking a three-pronged approach to secure fixity of tenure, fair rents and free sale of the interests of the tenants.

Over the next few years, Davitt's political activism rankled with the landlords and their political representatives and he had to endure short periods of incarceration for his outspoken views. But the intellectual power of his political

Michael Davitt statue (Photo: Davitt Museum)

Section 4

People and Places

Ashford Castle (Photo: MAYO.IE)

Foxford Woollen Mills, Mother Agnes and the River Moy

The River Moy helps define Foxford, a town of 1,300 people situated at the western edge of the Ox Mountains with Lough Conn, Lough Carra and Nephin mountain close by on its western flank. After its long, steady journey through Sligo and Mayo to the south of the Ox Mountains, the River Moy takes advantage of a gap at the end of the mountains to flow northwards through Straide and Foxford before continuing to Ballina and emptying into Killala Bay.

This water connection to the Atlantic Ocean is essential for the plentiful supply of salmon and sea trout that makes Foxford and its nearby lakes a favoured holiday and angling location for many overseas visitors and natives alike. The Moy is spanned by a narrow bridge in the centre of the town and is surrounded by a plentiful supply of bed and breakfasts, holiday rentals, pubs, cafes, restaurants and picturesque walking trails to cater for the needs of the visitor.

The River Moy played a significant part in the early development and subsequent expansion of the Foxford Woollen Mills (originally the Providence Woollen Mills) which opened in the town in 1892. Down the years the name Foxford has become synonymous worldwide with top quality woollen blankets, jackets, skirts, suits and other apparel. A pair of Foxford woollen blankets have become treasured wedding presents for thousands of new couples with subsequent generations keen to hold on to such family heirlooms.

The development of the Foxford Woollen Mills has much to thank for the chance alignment of a unique talent, a rich and powerful water supply, the migration of experienced weavers and craftsmen and the establishment of a convent in the town by the Sisters of Charity.

Foxford Woollen Mills and River Moy (Photo: Religious Sisters of Charity and Foxford Woollen Mills)

Mother Agnes
(Photo: Religious Sisters of Charity and Foxford Woollen Mills)

Mother Agnes Morrogh-Bernard was born in Cheltenham, Gloucesterhire in England in 1842, the daughter of an upper-class Irish Catholic, John Morrogh, who originally came from Glanmire in Cork and Hampshire-born mother, Frances Mary Blount. The family moved back to Ireland shortly after Agnes was born and lived in Cork till 1849. Her early years saw the worst excesses of the Great Famine in Ireland. In 1849, her father inherited the Bernard estates in County Kerry whereupon he hyphenated his surname to Morrogh-Bernard. Agnes had seven brothers and three sisters.

Agnes was deeply moved by the lot of the poor through starvation and poverty in the aftermath of the Great Famine in Ireland. This awareness imbued her with the desire to serve others especially the poor. Her parents were enlightened landlords and provided work opportunities for both men and women on their estates. After initial education at home by her mother, Agnes spent three years from 1854 – 1857 at Laurel Hill convent in Limerick followed by a short stint at a finishing school in Paris.

In 1863 at the age of twenty-one years, Agnes Morrogh-Bernard entered the Sisters of Charity convent in Harold's Cross as a postulant and was subsequently professed in January 1866, just short of her 24th birthday. Teaching posts in Dublin followed until 1877 when she was appointed Reverend Mother at a new convent in Ballaghaderreen. Mother Mary Arsenius Morrogh-Bernard, as she was known, established a fledgling spinning business as well as a school there soon after her arrival.

In 1890, after an approach from Bishop John Lyster of Achonry and a local police sergeant in Foxford, she and another sister moved into a house in Foxford and began the process of establishing a convent there. She quickly recognised the potential of the local River Moy and transferred her spinning and weaving operation from Ballaghaderreen to Foxford. Her business acumen saw her enlist the support of the Congested Districts Board, Sir Horace Plunkett, Fr Tom Kilroy S.J. and builder John Charles Smith from Caledon Mills, County Tyrone to help with construction of a Woollen Mill.

In 1892, the Providence Woollen Mills opened and immediately offered opportunities for employment to the locals. A school was established and was soon followed by the creation of the Foxford Brass and Reed Band in 1897. With increasing income, houses for the 100+ employees were built as well as a sophisticated road network to provide access to their homes. A music school followed in 1923 and then the convent chapel which was built in 1925.

Mother Morrogh-Bernard tended to avoid partisan politics but did act during the excesses of the Black and Tans resulting in convictions and penalties being applied for their actions. She is also credited with the building of the town's handball alley in 1901. There is no information available about her own abilities at handball but she did possess an eclectic range of talents, all well attuned to local community needs.

Mother Morrogh-Bernard was an inspirational success story for Foxford, transforming the town and the local community during her life-time. The Woollen Mills expanded and became more efficient all the while contributing to the local community and the economy. By 1905, the Woollen Mill products were available for purchase at leading Dublin stores, including Brown Thomas, Switzer's and Arnott's as well as through leading outlets throughout Ireland.

Exterior of Foxford Woollen Mills in Winter (Photo: Religious Sisters of Charity and Foxford Woollen Mills)

At the time of her death aged 90 years in 1932, Foxford Woollen Mills had firmly established its reputation for quality and this legacy has persisted to the present day. Foxford Woollen Mills were not immune to subsequent economic hardship and changes in the textile and fashion industries. In 1987, the business went into receivership only to be rescued in 1999 when it was taken over by a new design team. Substantial re-investment took place in 2007 with a focus on the visitor and holiday trade. The re-vitalised business now includes a visitor centre with multi-lingual tours of an operating woollen mill together with a shop showcasing its products and a restaurant to replenish lost energy.

Mother Agnes Morrogh-Bernard is buried in the local convent cemetery.

Foxford Woollen Mills Loom 1 (Photo: Religious Sisters of Charity and Foxford Woollen Mills)

Foxford Woollen Mills Loom 2 (Photo: Religious Sisters of Charity and Foxford Woollen Mills)

Louis Brennan – Torpedo Man

Louis Brennan and one of his inventios (Photo: Wikimedia Commons)

Not too many people outside his native County Mayo would be too familiar with the extraordinary inventions of Louis Brennan. Born in Castlebar in 1852, Louis was the tenth child of Thomas and Bridget Brennan, hardware merchants. Back then, Mayo and the rest of Ireland was attempting to recover from the decimation of the Great Famine. Ireland's population had halved in the space of a decade due to a combination of death through starvation or by emigration. Louis, then aged nine years, his parents and siblings followed the latter route and emigrated to Melbourne, Australia in 1861. Prospects must have been more appealing down there as it coincided with the Australian gold rush and places like Ballarat and the Central Victorian goldfields began yielding up the precious metal.

(The author (TB) worked in a solo medical practice in Dunolly, in the North Central Victorian goldfields area between 1985 and 1988. His first receptionist was the great, great, granddaughter of John Deason who became famous as one of the two men who discovered the Welcome Stranger, the largest gold nugget ever discovered in Australia. The nugget was too large to weigh on scales in Dunolly and had to be broken up into three pieces on a local blacksmith's anvil. It weighed over 2,500 ounces or 70kgs. It was very valuable then but in today's money probably over 2.7 million Euros).

After the Brennan family settled in Melbourne, the inventive skills of young Louis soon started to flourish. One of his jobs was as an apprentice to a watchmaker. His desire for further learning encouraged him to attend night classes in Collingwood's School of Design. In 1873, he had an eclectic range of exhibits including a billiard marker, a mincing machine and a safety latch at the Juvenile Industries Exhibition in Melbourne. His talent soon attracted the attention of other engineers. Industrialist Alexander Kennedy Smith took Louis under his wing and mentored his emerging talent.

Shortly after this at the age of 22 years, Louis began working on a prototype for what later emerged as one of the first controlled torpedoes ever invented. With Smith's support and encouragement, his protégé joined a local Volunteer Artillery Regiment in Victoria. One of the key areas under development at the time was the guided missile and its potential use both in defence and in warfare. Initial trials of Louis's new device showed it capable of accurately hitting a target over three kilometres away.

The Victorian government liked his work and in due course the Brennan Torpedo Company was formed. He was very conscious of the enormous potential of his invention and protected his interest therein by patenting the 'Brennan torpedo' in 1877. The climax of his development came with a test run in front of military and political leaders on Hobson Bay, near the mouth of the Yarra river in Melbourne. A significant contact at the time was fellow Irish-born Sir Andrew Clarke who held the key position as Inspector General of Fortifications in London. He invited Louis to present his invention to the War Office in London and his new invention was warmly welcomed.

His torpedo underwent rigorous testing under the Royal Engineers at Chatham and its potential to protect British ports and harbours was quickly realised. Trials were also conducted at Crosshaven at the entrance to Cork Harbour in 1884. Three years later, the British Government bought the patent from Louis for 110,000 pounds sterling – an estimated 11 million pounds sterling in today's money. To add some further cream, Louis was also appointed to the prestigious position of Superintendent of the Brennan torpedo factory at Gillingham in Kent on a salary of 1,500 pounds sterling per annum. He maintained his links with the facility till 1907 when improved gunnery started to replace his torpedo-based defence system.

Louis was honoured by royalty for his work and was made a Companion of the Order of the Bath in 1892 by Queen Victoria. His next big interest was a gyroscopically-balanced monorail system. He had a scaled down model developed and installed in the garden of his mansion in Gillingham in Kent. He saw this newest railway invention as intrinsically cheaper than the double rail system which had been spreading rapidly all over the world. As it was built on just one rail, it was much more manoeuvrable, especially around tight corners and on mountains, and it also provided a much more comfortable ride and travelled much faster than its double rail opposition.

Prime Minister Asquith took a ride on his monorail exhibit at the Japanese-British Exhibition in London in 1910 where it won the Grand Prize. Future Prime Minister Winston Churchill was also an enthusiastic supporter. But the press, parliamentarians and the conventional double-rail train industry continued to be sceptical of its safety. Many of Brennan's financial investors withdrew their support and he was ultimately destroyed financially and forced to sell his luxury house.

During the first world war, Louis was employed in the munitions industry where his expertise was harnessed to refine emerging, highly-secretive bombs. Churchill remained an ardent supporter and encouraged the Air Ministry to help further his plans for a working helicopter. In 1922 a prototype of Brennan's helicopter was given a public viewing and once again Louis did not disappoint. Much like the monorail, further development did not proceed and his ideas languished especially after 1925 when a prototype crashed and the Air Ministry withdrew funding. Louis made some further attempts to engage support for both the monorail and helicopter projects but despite investing a lot of his own finance, the outcome sadly ended with bankruptcy.

One of his major contributions to his native Ireland was his support in the founding of the National Academy of Ireland in 1922. Louis married fellow Castlebar native, Anna Quinn, in 1891 and they had two children. Anna was troubled by illness during her life and to enable her to get upstairs, Louis developed a chair lift to facilitate this.

Louis died in 1932 a few months after being injured in a motor vehicle accident in Switzerland and just short of his eightieth birthday. He was buried in an unmarked grave at St Mary's Cemetery in Kelsall Green, in London. In March 2014, fellow Mayo man and Taoiseach, Enda Kenny T.D. unveiled a new headstone in his honour. An exhibition of his life and work also took place at that time at the Mayo County Library in Castlebar.

HARRY CLARKE WINDOWS

Harry Clarke (Photo: Collection National Irish Visual Arts Library (NIVAL), NCAD, Dublin. Reproduced courtesy of De Búrca Rare Books)

Harry Clarke (1899 – 1931) is ranked in the pantheon of Ireland's stained-glass artists. Harry's father, Joshua (1859 – 1921), had moved to Dublin from Leeds in 1877 and married a Sligo girl, Brigid MacGonigle from Cliffony. Unfortunately, Brigid died from tuberculosis when Harry was only fourteen years old. Harry left school at Belvedere College and became apprenticed to his father's church decorating business. Harry studied glass staining at the Dublin Metropolitan School of Art winning Gold Medals from London on the way including one for his window in St Mel's Cathedral in Longford.

Harry's fame as an artist grew rapidly securing him numerous commissions for his work including illustrations for the publishers of 'Fairy Tales of Hans Christian Andersen' in 1916 and nine windows for the Honan Chapel at University College Cork in the period 1915 – 1918. He took over his father's stained-glass business in 1921 on the death of his father while another brother, Walter, concentrated on the church decorating business. Harry's reputation continued to flourish and commissions for work in Ireland (notably six in Bewley's café in Dublin and the Life of Christ windows in Diseart convent in Dingle), England, Switzerland, USA and Australia followed.

The Mayo connection for Harry Clarke's artistry centred around three prominent Mayo clergymen – Monsignor Thomas Shannon and Dean D'Alton at St Mary's Church in Ballinrobe as well as Canon MacDonald at St Patrick's Church in Newport. Nine of the windows in Ballinrobe were designed and created by Harry Clarke. Most people agree that his Last Judgement windows in Newport are the pinnacle of his work. Canon MacDonald reportedly cashed in his own life insurance policy to secure the artist's services such was his desire to have the master's work on permanent exhibition in his local church.

Poor health was a constant during Harry Clark's short, 41 years of life. Like his mother, he too got infected with tuberculosis in 1929 and died two years later in Switzerland where he sought fresh air and isolation to deal with the scourge of the then incurable disease. On his death, only one of the three windows commissioned for St Patrick's Church in Newport has been installed and poor Canon MacDonald was reported to have been distraught. The other two windows, designed by Harry, were completed and installed after his death by his company. One of the windows in the Last Judgement contains an image in green, reputedly a cameo of Harry himself, as one of the devils sliding down into hell! A close inspection is demanded on your next trip to Newport…

The Washing of the Feet, St. James's Church Charlestown
(Photo: Alan Johnson/Swinford Photography)

Our Lady and St Anthony St. James's Church Charlestown
(Photo: Alan Johnson/Swinford Photography)

There are some other original works by Clarke in County Mayo including St Patrick's Church in Kilmaine and The Ascension dated 1926 in the Church of the Immaculate Conception in Roundfort. A total of 160 windows throughout Ireland are regarded as true Harry Clarke originals including at St Patrick's Purgatory on Lough Derg.

Other churches in County Mayo containing examples of windows created under Clark's supervision and produced by his company include St Colman's in Claremorris, St Joseph's in Ballindine, St John the Baptist in Knock and St Mary of the Holy Rosary in Cong. Other church windows from his family company, Harry Clarke Stained Glass Ltd, can be found at St James's Church in Charlestown, Ballyhaunis Friary, St Thomas's Church in Callow, St Patrick's Church in Lahardane, Newport Oratory, St Mary's Church in Tooreen and St Mary's in Westport.

Some of the artist's own favourite commissions include a window for St Stephen's Cathedral in Brisbane, Australia installed in 1923 and another, a window for the International Labour Court in Geneva, depicting Irish literary scenes that was rejected by the Irish Government at the time as being too salacious! The latter window is now on permanent display at the Wolfsonian Institute in the University of Florida in Miami.

Our Lady and Christ the King St. James's Church Charlestown (Photo: Alan Johnson/Swinford Photography)

St Patrick's Church Newport Last Judgement (Photo: Tom Brett)

St Stephen's Cathedral (Photo: Brisbane Arch–diocese)

Cong and The Quiet Man

The picturesque village of Cong along the north-eastern shore of Lough Corrib straddles the Mayo-Galway border. It is an area well known for its iconic natural beauty and in 1951 was selected as the setting for the film 'The Quiet Man'. The arrival of film crews and the leading film stars of the day into Cong in the early 1950s changed the life of the village forever. The ensuing film production focussed the eyes of the world on Cong's idyllic rural location as seen through the medium of film using the newly invented Technicolor.

The film was directed by John Ford and represented a departure for him from his usual classic Westerns prior to this. The star cast was led by John Wayne, playing the part of Sean Thornton, a wealthy Irish-American who left his home in Pittsburgh to try to buy back the family home of his ancestors in County Mayo. Playing opposite him in the female lead was Maureen O'Hara as the fiery, red-head Mary Kate Danaher. Her brother, Will 'Red' Danaher, played by Victor McLaglen, was the local wealthy landowner and he too had an interest in purchasing the family farm sought by Thornton. The Widow Tillane, who was the current owner of the property, was played by Mildred Natwick. Other key characters were the local priest played by Ward Bond and the ubiquitous match-maker expertly played by Barry Fitzgerald.

The Quiet Man is famous for many classic scenes and draws fans of the film from around the world to Cong and its surrounds to retrace some of the sets and characters involved. These scenes include a prolonged fist-fight between Thornton and Will Danaher, horse racing at Lettergesh beach, a train scene at Ballyglunin station in County Galway, the White O'Morn cottage near Maam as well as the 'The Quiet Man Bridge' between Maam Cross and Oughterard. Some of the filming also took place in the grounds of Ashford Castle, adjacent to Cong.

Iaureen O'Hara, Victor McLaglen and John Wayne The Quiet Man (Photo: Wikimedia Commons)

John Ford is reported to have personally chosen some of the music melodies for the film including that of the 'Isle of Inisfree' which is reprised about a dozen times throughout the two hours plus production. Other traditional Irish tunes used include 'The Wild Colonial Boy' and the 'Rakes of Mallow'. The film is also noteworthy for the use of spoken Irish language, a rarity at the time in major international films.

The Quiet Man scooped Academy Awards for Best Director (John Ford) and Best Cinematography (Winton C Hoch and Archie Stout). The advent of modern digital technology has seen The Quiet Man become widely available in DVD and Blu-ray formats.

Maureen O'Hara listed The Quiet Man as her favourite film and before she died aged 95 years in 2015 is reported to have listened to the film's soundtrack in the days before her passing.

Not a bad way to go!

Ashford Castle

Princess Grace in Newport (Photo: Mayo Co Library)

Situated on the banks of Lough Corrib on the outskirts of Cong in County Mayo, Ashford Castle is one of the world's most prestigious hotels and holiday locations. It was voted 'Best Hotel in the World' in 2015 by leading international travel agencies. Over the years its iconic location and unique grandeur has brought Mayo to world attention. It received probably its biggest publicity ever when it hosted the stay of Prince Rainier and Princess Grace of Monaco during their historic state visit to Ireland in 1961.

Princess Grace had strong Mayo connections through her grandfather James Kelly from Drimurla, outside Newport, County Mayo who left Ireland for Philadelphia in 1887. Her father, John Kelly, represented the United States in rowing at the Olympic Games.

Grace Kelly was the leading screen star of her generation starring in movies such as High Noon with Gary Cooper in 1952; The Rear Window with James Stewart in 1954, and High Society with Bing Crosby and Frank Sinatra in 1956. The leading lady of screen stunned Hollywood when she bid farewell to her movie career and married the head of the Grimaldi family to became Princess Grace of Monaco on 18 April 1956.

Ashford Castle (Photo: MAYO.IE)

In earlier times, Ashford Castle was the location to host many of the stars and production team for the making of John Ford's The Quiet Man in 1951. The two leading stars of the movie, John Wayne and Maureen O'Hara, brought considerable interest and publicity to Cong's iconic hotel and surrounding countryside. King George V stayed there too while Prince of Wales back in 1905.

President Reagan stayed at Ashford Castle on his Irish roots trip in 1984 and has the Presidential suite dedicated to him. More recently, United Kingdom Prime Minister Tony Blair as well as John Lennon and George Harrison of the Beatles, Senator Ted Kennedy, Prince Edward, Brad Pitt, Pierce Brosnan, Rod Stewart and the Gallaghers of Oasis fame, have all shown their liking for the opulence that Ashford Castle has to offer.

In 2017, the roads and airspace around Cong were abuzz with arrivals to Ashford Castle of some of the leading sporting figures from around the globe for the wedding of Rory McIlroy and Erica Stoll. One of the sporting weddings of the year brought worldwide publicity to Cong and Ashford Castle. The close proximity of Ireland West Airport, Knock about 40 minutes away proved to be extremely convenient for those blessed with the luxury of private jet travel.

The original construction of Ashford Castle took place from about 1228 when the Anglo-Norman De Burgo family held sway in the West of Ireland. Their descendants, the Burkes, maintained ownership for over three centuries until their defeat and loss of estates in 1589. Sir Richard Bingham was President of Connacht at the time and took over control of the castle and its estate.

Subsequent owners in the late 17th Century were the Browne family followed by Sir Benjamin Guinness who bought it in 1852 from the Encumbered Estates Court in the aftermath of the Great Famine. Both Sir Benjamin and his son, Lord Ardilaun, were largely benevolent landlords who provided much needed employment in the locality. They extended the estate and were responsible for its upgrade including new gardens and widespread tree planting.

The Guinness family remained in control of Ashford Castle up until 1939 when ownership was transferred to the Irish Government. The Forestry Department held on to about 1200 hectares of the Ashford Castle estate (the Cong Forest part) but transferred ownership of the Castle and surrounding lands to Waterville hotelier, Noel Huggard, who developed the property into the luxury hotel we have become acquainted with today.

Irish-American John Mulcahy bought Ashford Castle in 1970 and doubled its size as well as developing the nine-hole golf course and gardens. Subsequent owners included Irish and American tycoons, including Tony O'Reilly and Chuck Feeney, and the Barrett family from Galway. After going into receivership, Ashford Castle estate was bought in 2013 by the Red Carnation Hotel group from South Africa who undertook further extensive renovations and upgrading of the hotel and grounds.

Ashford Castle and its grounds provide a unique example of the up-market, luxury market that visitors to this historic part of south Mayo can savour on their travels.

Ashford Castle (Photo: MAYO.IE)

SEAN FREYNE

Sean Freyne (Photo: K Finnerty)

Sean Freyne is a name that is synonymous with Mayo Gaelic Football and theology. As a sportsman and academic, Sean was often noted to quote from Plato 'the barbarians do not engage in sport or philosophy'. He was particularly keen to point out that sport came before philosophy in that very poignant quotation.

Born in Kilkelly, Co Mayo where his mother was a primary school teacher, Sean Freyne lost his father when he was just four years old. His mother built a house in nearby Tooreen, continued her primary teaching there and raised Sean and his sister, Mary. After primary school days, Sean attended St Jarlath's College in Tuam, a well know GAA nursery. His talents as a gaelic footballer developed and by his final year Sean was appointed captain of the Mayo minor team for the All Ireland Championship in 1953.

The Mayo minor team that year was recognised as one of the best. Mayo duly won the Connacht crown and secured their place in September's final by beating Armagh (5 goals and 2 points to 1 goal and 5 points) in the All Ireland semi-final. A spanner in the works occurred in early September when Sean decided to pursue his vocation of becoming a Catholic priest and entered St Patrick's College in Maynooth as a seminarian. Church rules at the time were much stricter and Sean was prohibited from leading his fellow Mayo minors onto the hallowed grounds of Croke Park for the All Ireland final.

Eamonn Walsh from Charlestown was promoted as Captain in Sean's absence and duly led Mayo to a convincing Minor final triumph over Clare (2 goals and 11 points to 1 goal and 6 points). Sean never expressed any bitterness on missing out on the big day. Many of his fellow county men and women were not so forgiving and the event, like a few others, is now part of Mayo's unique GAA footballing folklore.

In 1960, Sean was ordained a priest for the Tuam Archdiocese but instead of pursuing parish work, Sean was sent to Rome to further his ecclesiastical and theological studies. After a few years in Rome, Sean retuned to Ireland first to St Columban's College in Dalgan, Co Meath and later as Professor of Sacred Scripture at St Patrick's College in Maynooth from 1974 to 1976.

Sean left the priesthood in 1976. He later fell in love with and married an Australian lawyer, Gail Grossman. Their union subsequently produced two daughters, Bridget and Sarah, and the family lived mostly between Ireland and Australia. His academic career subsequently included teaching stints at the University of Queensland in Brisbane, Notre Dame University in Indiana and Loyola University in New Orleans.

In 1981, Sean Freyne found his ultimate academic theological niche with his appointment as foundation Chair of non-denominational Theology at Trinity College in Dublin. This was quite a departure for theological studies in Ireland at the time and a significant move away from church dominance in the field. Sean's major theological publications include the seminal works of (i) Galilee – from Alexander the Great to Hadrian, published in 1980, and (ii) Jesus a Jewish Galilean – a new reading of the Jesus story, published in 2004.

In 2007, Sean was appointed as Visiting Professor of Early Christian History at Harvard Divinity School. The appointment prompted the very apt Mayo News headline at the time – 'Tooreen man appointed visiting Professor at Harvard'. But why not!

Sean later established and directed the Centre for Mediterranean and Near Eastern Studies. After his retirement, he maintained an active interest in academia, led many groups on visits to the Holy Land and was an Emeritus Professor of Theology at Trinity College Dublin. He was also a Member of the Royal Irish Academy and a trustee of the Chester Beatty Library in Dublin.

Sean Freyne's lifelong interest in sport especially gaelic football coupled with his gregarious nature meant that he was ever present when Mayo football teams took the field. He instilled a passion for the green and red of Mayo in his family with daughters Bridget and Sarah fondly recalling attending matches with their father in all kinds of weather and in all parts of Ireland.

Sean Freyne died on 5 August 2013. He had witnessed many close calls for Mayo in All Ireland series in his final years and always maintained a firm belief that their day would come. President Mary McAleese described Sean as 'the quintessential Irishman… always asking the probing question'.

After his funeral mass at the Church of Our Lady Refuge of Sinners in Rathmines, celebrated by fellow Mayo man and life-long friend, Fr Enda McDonagh, Sean was laid to rest in Culmore graveyard near Kilkelly, Co Mayo. As befitted the occasion and the man, his coffin was draped in the green and red colours of Mayo.

Sarah Freyne (Photo: Tom Brett)

In the weeks after Professor Sean Freyne's passing, good friend and former Trinity student Kevin Finnerty from Castlecoote House in Roscommon recalled the "very great loss to his family, the academic world, his wide circle of friends, he GAA community and Irish society as a whole."

"A giant of a man in every respect. A great, great friend, a mentor, a trusted colleague and a teacher who always wanted to drag you up from the low road to the high road. In the academic world a colossus, nationally and internationally whose breadth of knowledge spanned realms and whose achievements in this regard are without parallel. A priest, a preacher, a rabbi, a rebel, a missionary, a maitreya who transcended religious divides. A teacher in the true traditional sense who did not limit his world view to matters theological, but extended it to a moral, social, political and cultural compasses as well.

Eamonn and Gillian Walsh and Kieran Mahon (Photo: Liam Lyons Collection)

Indeed, he could teach almost anything, I remember once asking him after he translated a chapter in the Latin Vulgate bible into both Hebrew and Greek, pointing out as he often did the similarities in these languages with our own Irish language. 'How many languages can you actually speak, Seán?' To which he replied 'I'm badly fluent in 10 of them!'

The world or matrix of the texts behind the stories in the Bible were his ongoing challenge and when embarking on the four-year Hebrew, Biblical and Theological studies in Trinity College Dublin, he instructed us to always carry a newspaper in one hand, the Bible in the other, demonstrating that we shape not our world around the Bible - rather our task was could we fashion the bible into our world at all.

"Great Caesar fell. And Oh what a fall was there my countrymen and I and you and all of us fell down......" that vast expanse of knowledge, that wonderful wisdom, the absolute integrity, alas now no more. All gone, buried on a hilltop overlooking a tree lined valley in the same grave as his dear father and mother in his native Kilkelly in his beloved Co. Mayo. A knowledge though that will continue to weave its way in this world, as he disseminated it with such joy to all lucky enough to cross his path and who remain his happy acolytes.

Ní bheidh a leithéid ann arís."

The annual Percy French school at Castlecoote in July hosts the Sean Freyne Memorial Lecture as its Thursday centrepiece. Well worth a visit!

Yes indeed, Sean Freyne was the quintessential Mayo man. It was good to know him.

Margaret Burke-Sheridan (Maggie from Mayo)

Margaret Burke-Sheridan (Photo: Copyright the biography of Margaret Burke-Sheridan, La Sheridan - Adorable Diva by Anne Chambers)

Known fondly as Maggie from Mayo, Margaret Burke-Sheridan became Ireland's Prima Donna during a very successful operatic singing career. She was born on the Mall in Castlebar, the youngest of five children to the local postmaster and his wife. Tragically by the age of 11 years both her parents had passed away and the orphaned Margaret found herself in care of the Sisters at the Dominican Convent in Eccles Street in Dublin. It was here that Mother Clement recognised her unique vocal talents and provided the initial singing lessons. At the 1908 Dublin Feis Ceoil, Margaret won a gold medal for singing in the music competition.

After this initial success and supported by some local fundraising, twenty-year-old Margaret went to the Royal Academy in London in 1909. During her London years, she had a chance meeting there with Marconi of telephone invention fame. He was enthralled with the quality of her voice and assisted her with opportunities to further her operatic career in Italy. After auditioning with the highly respected Alfredo Martino, Margaret soon achieved a significant operatic breakthrough. In January 1918 she had a very successful debut at the Teatro Constanzi as Mimi in Puccini's La Boheme. Her fame spread quickly and she appeared in the title role in Mascagni's Iris at the Royal Opera House in Covent Garden in July 1919.

Her success in Italy continued apace with starring roles at Milan's Teatro Del Varme and at the Teatro del Carlo in Naples. Another major break came in 1922 when she appeared at La Scala in Milan in Catalani's La Wally, directed by Toscanini. Her career in Italy subsequently included eight seasons at La Scala while Covent Garden was graced by her appearance over five seasons. The pinnacle of her career is seen as her performances in Madame Butterfly, some of which are reported to have beguiled even the great Puccini himself. Not a bad compliment for Maggie from Mayo!

In 1929-1930, Margaret Burke-Sheridan made a gramophone recording of the complete Madame Butterfly opera where she is accompanied by the La Scala orchestra. She made numerous other operatic recordings, both solos and duets, from the works of Verdi, Wagner, Puccini and Balfe. She extended her style to include some traditional Irish songs including compositions by Thomas Moore (Moore's Melodies) and an old favourite, Balfe's 'I dreamt I dwelt in marble halls'. Interestingly, Margaret never performed professionally in Ireland or in the United States.

Margaret Burke-Sheridan stamp (Photo: An Post)

In the mid-1930s, she developed problems with her voice and only made rare concert appearances after that. Rumours were that her career demise was in parallel with unfulfilled romantic encounters including one with an Italian count and another with the married Managing Director of the Royal Opera House in Covent Garden, Eustace Blois.

Margaret never married and retired to live in Dublin in her later years. She lived in an apartment on Fitzwilliam Street with occasional forays to the Shelbourne Hotel with patrons and friends. In her last years she developed cancer and lived at the Pembroke Nursing Home in Leeson Street where she died on 16 April 1958, aged 67 years.

Margaret Burke-Sheridan, Ireland's Prima Donna, is buried in Glasnevin Cemetery. The Margaret Burke-Sheridan competition at Dublin's annual Feis Ceoil is still held in her honour.

Margaret Burke-Sheridan with Vincenzo Bellezza, London, 1938 (Photo: Wikimedia Commons)

MARTIN SHERIDAN – MAYO'S FAMOUS OLYMPIAN

When Martin Sheridan from Bohola, County Mayo died in St Vincent's Hospital in Manhattan on 27 March 1918, he was just one day short of his 37th birthday. For such a fit, young man to succumb to the effects of the 1918 Spanish Flu pandemic in New York is scarcely credible by today's health standards. An obituary in the New York Times on 28 March 1918 reflected on Sheridan's outstanding athletic career citing him as one of the 'greatest athletes the United States has even known.'

In his youth Martin Sheridan possessed a fine athletic physique – weighing in at 88 kg and standing 191 cms or 6 foot 3 inches tall. Even in his youthful days around his native Bohola, Martin was noted for his strength and prowess especially in throwing events. After moving to the United States, he found employment with the New York Police Department like many of his fellow countrymen before and since. He soon became a regular member of the Irish American Athletic Club.

Martin Sheridan, Bohola's Olympian (Photo: Wikimedia Commons)

His most outstanding athletic achievements include gold medals for Discus throwing at the 1904 Olympic Games in St Louis and at the 1908 London Olympics where he also won another gold for the Greek Discus throw. Another event that is no longer an Olympic event – the Standing Long Jump – saw Sheridan win a bronze medal at the London Games in 1908.

In 1906, a special Olympics called the 'Intercalated Games' was held in Athens and Sheridan won gold in both the Shot Putt and Discuss throw as well as silver in three other (now defunct) events - the Standing Long Jump, the Standing High Jump and the Stone Throw. Martin Sheridan's total Olympic haul is an astonishing nine medals – five gold, three silver and one bronze. Not bad for a lad from Bohola, County Mayo!

Two of Martin's gold medals from the 1904 St Louis Olympics and the 1906 Intercalated games in Athens are on display in the USA Track and Field's Hall of Fame History Gallery located in Washington Heights at the top end of Manhattan in New York. Perhaps, it might inspire you to visit the exhibit and reflect on the glory the man from County Mayo brought to his adopted USA on the athletic field. A pity his native Ireland never got to reap the rewards of his Olympic medals.

Martin Sheridan is buried in Calvary Cemetery in Queens, New York.

Martin Sheridan - Bohola's Olympian (Photo: Mayo.IE)

ADMIRAL WILLIAM BROWN – ARGENTINE HERO

Admiral Brown Memorial Foxford (Photo: Tom Brett)

Admiral William Brown, born in Providence Street, Foxford in June 1777 is regarded as a national hero in Argentina and recognised as the founder of the Argentinian navy. He and his family emigrated to the United States when he was just nine years old and settled in the Philadelphia area. Soon after their arrival there, both his father and a family friend who was instrumental in the family moving to the United States, died from an outbreak of yellow fever.

Information on Brown's early life in the United States is scarce but a chance meeting with a merchant ship's captain along the banks of the Delaware River is recorded as paving the way for him to pursue a naval career. After some years on the high seas, he gradually progressed to the role of captain and ultimately had charge of his own ship. At the time the Napoleonic wars were taking place and William ended up incarcerated in French prisons on a few occasions.

In 1809, Brown returned to South America, first to Montevideo in Uruguay, where he traded between that country and Argentina. After the loss of a ship, he went for a while to Chile before returning with enough funds to buy another vessel and soon resumed his trading between Uruguay and Argentina. The Spanish were not too enamoured with this new local threat to their financial interests and soon destroyed his schooner. Argentina recognised this ongoing Spanish threat and enlisted the services of Brown and his selected comrades to help safeguard Argentinian interests. His leadership qualities soon became evident and his vessels freed the strategic River Plate from Spanish control and Argentina succeeded in capturing Montevideo.

After his successes over the Spanish, Brown took time out from naval pursuits and turned to farming and family life in Argentina for the following fourteen years. Then in 1825, with the outbreak of war Brazil attempted to blockade Argentina. Brown's experience and leadership was sought by Argentine leaders to command a new squadron of ships to take on the Brazilian navy. After a series of notable naval victories, Brown was nominated as the Argentinian commissioner to oversee the peace process that devolved following the Treaty of Montevideo in October 1827.

Towards the end of his life, Brown visited his native Foxford in 1847 in the middle of the Great Famine. He was aged 70 years at the time and was accompanied by his daughter. After his death on 3 March 1857, he was buried with full military hours. Tributes at the time stated that Admiral Brown 'symbolized the glory of the Argentine Republic' and his value when on the quarterdeck of one of his battleships was 'worth a fleet to us'.

It is estimated that over a thousand streets throughout Argentina are named after William Brown while the Plaza de Mayo is one of the major squares in Buenos Aires. Numerous soccer teams in Argentina as well as naval frigates and other

Admiral William Brown statue Foxford (Photo: W Brown Society)

vessels are named after him. Commemorative stamps in his honour were issued by the Irish Government in 1957 while Argentina has also similarly honoured him.

Foxford has a museum in his honour while both Dublin and Foxford have statues erected in his memory. In November 2012, the Admiral Brown Cup was commissioned as the prize to be presented to the winning team in Ireland versus Argentina rugby matches. An annual commemorative parade in Foxford involving contingents of Argentine and Irish naval personnel as well as members of the diplomatic corps celebrate the great man's historical past and his links to both countries.

Admiral William Brown, Foxford native, is buried in La Recoleta Cemetery in Buenos Aires. His gravestone is coloured green.

Captain Juan Carlos Romay Argentine Navy Foxford (Photo: W Brown Society)

Oliver Murphy, Lt Commander Alan Flynn, Irish Naval Servic and Brendan Brett, Foxford (Photo: W Brown Society)

Argentine Naval Contingent, Admiral Brown commemoration, Foxford, Nov 2019 (Photo: W Browm Society)

Knock Shrine

Knock Shrine (Photo: PM photography and AD Wejchert Architects)

The Marian Shrine at Knock has attracted millions of pilgrims over the decades with hundreds of thousands continuing to flock to the place where the Blessed Virgin appeared to fifteen people from the village on August 21, 1879.

The Apparition which included St John the Evangelist, a Lamb and a cross on an altar took place at the gable wall of the Parish Church. The visionaries ranged in age from five to 74 years. Each of them testified at a Commission of Inquiry in October 1870 and their evidence was found to be trustworthy and satisfactory. A second Commission of Inquiry in 1936 again heard from the surviving witnesses who confirmed their original evidence.

For the past 140 years, Knock Shrine has been a source of comfort and hope for thousands of pilgrims. In the Summer months of the 1950s, 1960s and 1970s, the roads to Knock on Sundays were filled with hundreds of buses making their way to the shrine. The Sligo to Galway Road saw thousands of pilgrims from the north and west of Ireland navigating a much less sophisticated road network through Charlestown and on to Kilkelly and Knock.

Many cures have been recorded at the shrine and hand-written letters, crutches and sticks left by people claiming to be cured are to be seen at Knock Museum. Housed also at the Museum is the collection of testimonies given by the visionaries from 1879.

Marion Carroll had been ill for seventeen years with multiple sclerosis. She was incapacitated, the power drained from her limbs, her eyesight and speech diminished. She was confined to a wheelchair. She was at death's door when asked by a local ambulance driver if she would like to be taken to Knock. She felt too ill to make the journey but was persuaded by her husband, an army sergeant, who offered to stay home to mind their kids.

In the basilica they placed her on a stretcher under the statue of Our Lady. She prayed to the mother of God: "You are my mother too, you know how I feel," she pleaded.

Lying on the stretcher in St John's Home after the ceremony the wife of the doctor who had travelled with them to the shrine came to talk to her. Marion became emotional and asked her "would you think me stupid if I said I thought I could walk?"

The woman called a nurse. The stretcher was opened. Marion swung out her legs and stood up. "After all those years I was not even stiff. My speech was perfect, my hands and arms were perfect," she said.

A visit to Knock Shrine was one of the major goals of the first ever visit to Ireland of a reigning Pontiff when Pope John Paul II visited in 1979. Thousands attended the open-air Mass. In August 2018, Pope Francis also celebrated Mass at the shrine on his visit to Ireland.

On 1 September 2019 during a pilgrimage to Knock Shrine, Archbishop Michael Neary of Tuam confirmed the Catholic Church's position that Marion Carroll had been cured during a visit there in 1989. 'Thirty years ago on the occasion of this pilgrimage, Marion was healed here at Our Lady's Shrine. Today the Church formally acknowledges that this healing does not admit of any medical explanation and joins in prayer, praise and thanksgiving to God.' Marion Carroll was present for the announcement and the news made national and international headlines.

Knock Basilica (Photo: PM photography and AD Wejchert Architects)

Knock Basilica Mosaic (Photo: PM Photgraphy)

ROSARY PRIEST - FR PATRICK PEYTON

Fr Peyton, Princess Grace (Photo: Fr Peyton Memorial Centre)

Known affectionately as the 'Rosary Priest', Fr Patrick Peyton was born in 1909 in Attymass, County Mayo in the shadows on the Ox Mountains. He was the sixth eldest of nine children born to John and Mary Peyton. The family rosary was an everyday part of the Peyton family life and it is this devotion to the rosary that sparked his lifelong crusade and message 'the family that prays together, stays together.'

Unfortunately, opportunities for members of large families residing on small holdings in Mayo in the early decades of the 20th century were few and far between. The emigrant route was often the only genuine chance for a better life. Three of his sisters had already crossed the Atlantic to Pennsylvania when 19 years old Patrick and his brother Thomas followed them in 1928. The family's devotion to the church remained strong and Patrick became a church sexton before both he and his brother decided to enter the seminary and train for the priesthood.

Fr Peyton Bing Crosby (Photo: Fr Peyton Memorial Centre)

Galway Ballybrit Racecourse Rally 1954 (Photo: Fr Peyton Memorial Centre)

Along the way, Patrick became infected with tuberculosis but managed to make a good recovery at the cost of 12 months in hospital. Both brothers were ordained priests in June 1941. Fr Patrick subsequently worked for a year in New York as a chaplain. After that 12 months chaplaincy work and with the support of the church, he began undertaking his life time goal of promoting the family rosary and family values throughout the United States and in many parts of the world.

In the succeeding years, Fr Peyton became adept at using his keen communication skills to spread his message with the assistance of the media and some of theatre's star performers. In 1947 in Hollywood, he established Family Theatre Productions and he used this connection to produce thousands of newspaper articles as well as radio and television programs over the years.

Fr Peyton visited Ireland in 1954 and attracted over 20,000 to one of his meetings at Knock. The Irish Independent carried a weekly article about the power of the rosary and the importance of family values. He continued his rosary crusade for the next thirty years often addressing large meetings in countries all over the globe.

Fr Patrick Peyton died aged 83 years on 3 June 1992 and is buried in East Easton, near Boston in Massachusetts. Today, Attymass honours one of its most famous sons with the Father Patrick Peyton Memorial Centre located in the village.

The Centre opened in 1998 and contains both audio and visual recordings of Fr Peyton's life's work including some highlighting his extraordinary ability to harvest the talents of supportive Hollywood and Broadway talent of his era to facilitate his own missionary zeal to promote the importance of the family rosary and family life. Prominent acquaintances at the time who supported him included Bing Crosby, Grace Kelly, Gregory Peck and Frank Sinatra.

The Attymas Fr Peyton Memorial Centre offers a rich array of facilities including a peace garden, meeting rooms, bed and breakfast accommodation, catering for adult and student retreats as well as other visiting groups, all in peaceful surroundings located in the shadow of the Ox mountains between Swinford and Foxford. It is well worth a visit on your next trip to Mayo.

Fr Peyton Memorial Centre, Attymass

FAMOUS PEOPLE WITH MAYO CONNECTIONS

Böll Cottage Achill exterior (Photo: John Michael Nikolai)

Heinrich Böll

Heinrich Böll was a regular visitor to Ireland and lived for a time in his cottage at Dugort on Achill Island. He was awarded the Nobel Prize for literature in 1972. His observations on island life on Achill provide sociological insights into family life there with poverty and recurrent emigration two of the dominant themes in some of his writings. His Irish Journal (Irisches Tagebuck) captures the essence of rural life in Ireland in the 1950s. Böll died in 1985. There is a memorial in his honour at Keel, Achill Island.

Sir Ernest Chain (Photo: MAYO.IE)

Sir Ernest Chain

Professor Sir Ernest Chain was a world famous, German-born biochemist of Jewish descent who opted to leave his homeland for Britain in 1933 with the rise of Nazism. After an outstanding career at both Cambridge and Oxford, he collaborated with the Australian physician, Howard Florey, to tease out the earlier work of Alexander Fleming, discoverer of penicillin, as to how the revolutionary new antibiotic worked its magic. Florey studied the therapeutic properties of penicillin while Chain laid out its biochemistry. For their outstanding contribution to medicine, Fleming, Chain and Florey were awarded the Nobel Prize in 1945. After World War 11 in 1945, Chain learned that his mother and sister had not survived the Jewish holocaust.

Sir Ernest and Lady Chain loved to visit Mayo. In 1970 the couple came to live in their newly constructed cottage at Mulranny. In 1979, Sir Ernest's health deteriorated and he died at Castlebar General Hospital in August. The author had the honour of caring for him in his final illness and with completing his death certificate. Chain was an outstanding scientist who was respected all over the world. The biochemistry building in Oxford is named after him while Castlebar has also named a street in his honour.

Jack Charlton (Photo: Wikimedia Commons)

Jack Charlton

Few foreign-born sportsmen have been shown as much adulation as Jack Charlton received during his glorious reign as the Irish soccer manager in the period 1986 – 1996. During those ten years, the Republic of Ireland qualified for the European Championships in 1988 and that was followed by a first World Cup appearance in Italy 1990 when Ireland played in a pool including England and Romania and made it to the quarter-finals. Over 500,000 turned out in Dublin to welcome Jack Charlton and the team back home!

In 1994, the Republic of Ireland had to survive two tough matches against Northern Ireland before successfully qualifying for the World Cup finals in the United States. In their first pool match against one of the top teams, Italy, a Ray Houghton goal brought victory to Ireland and sent the country into ecstasy. Italy went to win the World Cup but, sadly, Ireland failed to progress beyond the group stage.

Jack Charlton loved fishing and soon fell in love with Ballina and fishing opportunities on the Moy. Together with his wife Pat, he bought a house at Moy Heights overlooking the river in 1991. He became a regular feature on the streets of Ballina, at his favourite fishing spots and the occasional venture into the local Ballina pubs. His love of fishing and his positive comments on the richness of the Moy basin provided a boost for tourism in Mayo and throughout Ireland.

Jack eventually sold the holiday house in Ballina as he considered the maintenance too onerous for the couple's advancing years. He still maintained his contact with the area and returned twice a year for salmon fishing. As a player who scaled the heights with a World Cup win in 1966 together with his younger brother, Bobby, and who won the English Championship with Leeds United, he always possessed the innate ability to relax and enjoy the company of friends at all levels. But his days as the Irish soccer manager built that relationship to an entirely different level.

Mayo rightly honours Jack Charlton as one of our most famous adopted sons.

Jackie Clarke Centre in Ballina (Photo: Mayo Co. Library)

Jackie Clarke

Jackie Clarke (1927 – 2000) was a Ballina native who during his life as a businessman and local politician became a keen collector of an eclectic range of memorabilia, historical books, pamphlets, political cartoons and posters, documents, maps and photographs. Historical items of note include an original Easter Rising Proclamation from 1916, letters and other memorabilia from Michael Collins, Theobald Wolfe Tone, Michael Davitt, O'Donovan Rossa and Douglas Hyde.

After his death, his wife Anne gifted the entire Jackie Clarke Collection in 2005 to Mayo County Council and Ireland.

The former Provincial Bank in Pearse Street Ballina was acquired to house the collection which was officially opened to the public in June 2015. The old bank building has its own history being designed by the renowned architect Thomas Deane and opening in 1881. Other famous buildings designed by Deane include the National Museum in Dublin and Government Buildings. The Ballina building served as a bank until 1971 and underwent a complete refurbishment to accommodate the collection.

The Jackie Clarke Collection is open from Tuesday to Saturday and is well worth a visit on your next trip to the Ballina area.

Cardinal John D'Alton (Photo: Armagh Archdiocese)

Cardinal D'Alton

John Francis D'Alton (1882 – 1963) was born in Claremorris and after national school locally attended Blackrock College and later Clonliffe's Holy Cross College. At Blackrock, he befriended Eamonn De Valera who was also a student there at the time. He was ordained to the priesthood in Rome in 1908 and subsequently undertook higher theological studies at Cambridge and Oxford prior to his appointment in 1910 to St Patrick's College in Maynooth. During his time there, he taught Ancient Classics, Latin and Greek and maintained a strong interest in history. He became President of Maynooth from 1936 to 1942 before progressing to become Bishop of Meath in 1943. He became Primate of All Ireland in 1946 on his appointment as Archbishop of Armagh following the death of Cardinal MacRory. He was subsequently appointed a Cardinal in January 1953 by Pope Pius X11. The previous year, he became the first member of the Irish Hierarchy to receive an honorary degree from Queen's University in Belfast when he was awarded a Doctorate in Literature.

Cardinal D'Alton played a key role in the preparations for the Second Vatican Council called by Pope John XX111 and was the leader of the Irish Hierarchy group that attended the first session in 1962. He died of a heart attack in Dublin in February 1963 and was interred in the grounds of St Patrick's Cathedral in Armagh.

ard Delaney on River Liffey (Photo: Collection NIVAL NCAD Reproduced courtesy of Delaney Family)

Edward Delaney

Edward Delaney (1930 - 2009) was born in Crossboyne, near Claremorris, and during his lifetime became one of Ireland's most respected sculptors. He studied at the National College of Art and Design and later gained experience with castings in Germany.

His major works include the Tomas Davis statue opposite Trinity College Dublin from 1966 followed by the Theobald Wolfe Tone statue and nearby Famine Memorial from 1967 at the north-eastern section of St Stephen's Green in Dublin. Other notable pieces from his life's work include Eve with Apple from 1958 in the Museum of Modern Art in Dublin and a large six metre Celtic Twilight piece located on the campus of University College Dublin.

Edward Delaney is buried with his parents in the family plot in Crossboyne cemetery. His family erected his stainless-steel globe sculpture, Integration, in a garden adjoining the Sacred Heart Church in Crossboyne in 2013.

ard Delaney sculpture Ceathru Rua (Photo: John Fallon)

Paul Durcan (Photo: Tourism Ireland)

Paul Durcan

Paul Durcan is one of Ireland's leading poets and has strong Mayo connections. Born in Dublin to a Barrister father and a Mayo mother with links to Major John McBride and Maud Gonne, Paul spent a lot of his young days in the Westport and Turlough areas. His mother's sister owned a pub in Turlough and his visits there are reflected in his poetry. His eponymous 'Going home to Mayo, Winter, 1949' reflects his connections with Mayo and Ireland's rural heartland.

His Mayo links are found in his 1975 work 'O Westport in the Light of Asia Minor' published a year after receiving the Patrick Kavanagh Poetry award. He was the London Poetry Book Society choice in 1985 for one of his most famous works 'The Berlin Wall Café'. In 1990 he was awarded both the Whitbread Prize for 'Daddy, Daddy' and the Irish Times Irish Literature Prize for Poetry. In recognition of his outstanding contribution to his craft, Paul Durcan was appointed Ireland's third professor of poetry in 2004.

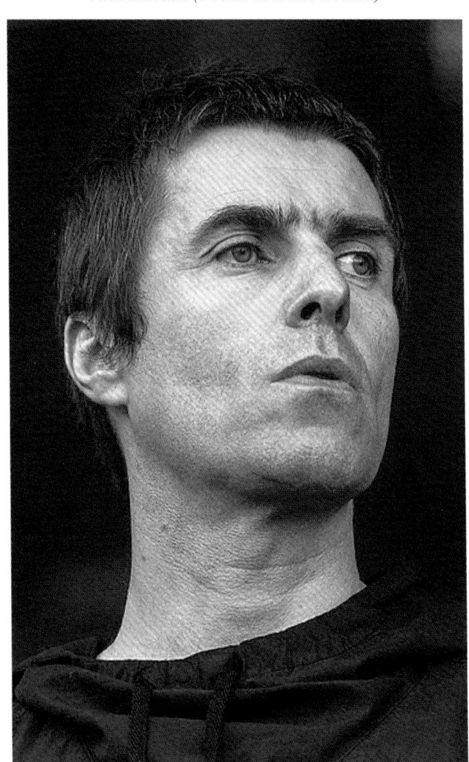

Liam Gallagher
(Photo: Stefan Bending, Creative Commons, SA Germany)

Liam and Noel Gallagher

Former Oasis leads, Noel and Liam Gallagher, were born in the Burnage area of Manchester but have resolutely maintained their strong Mayo connections. Their mother, Peggy (nee Sweeney) was born in the Culmore area outside Charlestown and the boys were regular visitors to their grandmother's home in their youth.

Local Charlestown publican and hardware merchant, John Finan, knew both Liam and Noel long before fame and fortune came their way. Always a man with a keen ear for musical talent, John recalls the time the brothers made their first CD. 'Nobody had heard of them before that but after a few weeks they were in the Top 10 over in England.' The Oasis era had arrived and the Gallaghers suddenly became international superstars with millions of record sales.

When their grandmother, Margaret Sweeney died in September 2012 both Noel and Liam attended the funeral services in Charlestown and mixed with some of the locals in the graveyard and at a reception in KD's pub afterwards.

Liam Gallagher has attributed a re-kindling of his interest in music to a further visit to the Charlestown area and an impromptu session in Finan's pub in 2015.

Brendan Graham

Brendan Graham

Brendan Graham is one of Ireland's leading song-writers and his compositions have been recorded by artists of all musical genres with more than 100 million copies sold to date. His best-known work 'You Raise Me Up' ranks as one of the most successful songs of all time with recordings by about a thousand artists across 40 different languages.

This inspiring composition has been a signature feature of many national and international events including the Olympic Games, Opening of the Northern Ireland Assembly, the 1916 Easter Rising Centenary Concert, Nobel Prize presentations, White House events, Queen Elizabeth's historic visit to Ireland, Pope Francis in the United States as well the official Ground Zero commemorations in New York.

Recording artists who have recorded his works include Aretha Franklin, Johnny Matthis, Andre Rieu, The Chieftains, Tommy Fleming, Rita Coolidge, Katherine Jenkins, Russell Watson, Kate Ceberano, Aled Jones and the Mormon Tabernacle Choir.

His 'Isle of Hope, Isle of Tears' has a direct link to County Mayo as it records the journey of 16-year- old Mayo-born Annie Moore, the first person through the gates of Ellis Island on her arrival in America in 1943. These lyrics have been widely quoted in both academic publications and in the popular media and have been incorporated into the teaching syllabus for American history in some states.

Ireland's last two Eurovision Song Contest successes – 'Rock and Roll Kids' performed by Paul Harrington and Charlie McGettigan in 1994 and 'The Voice' sung by Eimear Quinn in 1996 – were both written by Brendan Graham.

Born in County Tipperary, Graham trained as an industrial engineer and worked in both Ireland and Australia. He was capped for Ireland in basketball at youth level and captained the Monash University rugby team in Melbourne.

On returning to Ireland, he devoted himself full time to his music and song writing. He has been described as 'a musical midas' by the Irish Times and 'having a touch of genius' by Con Houlihan of the Evening Herald. These descriptions aptly capture his unique talent and worldwide appeal. Brendan Graham has now settled in County Mayo where he and his family enjoy the quiet inspiration provided by our mountains, rivers and lakes. Long may his output continue!

John Healy

John Healy (1930 – 1991) was born in Charlestown and in his day became one of the most prominent political and social commentators in Irish journalism. His initial cadetship in 1948 was with the Western People in Ballina. He later moved to Dublin and worked with the Irish News Agency, the Irish Press, the Evening Press and the Irish Times where Douglas Gageby was a good friend.

John Healy (Photo: Healy Family)

His trademark journalistic work will always be his Backbencher column for the Irish Times. He had excellent political contacts and an uncanny ability to express his thoughts succinctly in his daily and weekly columns. He won the RTE Jacob's Award for TV scriptwriting in the Headlines and Deadlines progamme before progressing to hosting 'Hurler on the Ditch' on RTE Television.

One of the biggest causes that Healy espoused was the revolutionary free education proposals from Donough O'Malley in 1967. This sea-change in Irish education saw free school buses introduced, free secondary schooling as well as a grants scheme for University education. These changes had a profound effect on Irish communities, especially many in rural areas.

Students could now aspire to attend University and would be grant assisted on reaching a minimum of four honours in their Leaving Certificate examination. It may look modest in today's economic times but in the late 1960s this plan transformed the Irish education landscape. John Healy was unstinting in his praise for the vision shown by Donough O'Malley in introducing these innovative changes.

O'Malley's sudden death at only 47 years in March robbed Healy of one of his greatest political contacts and heroes while the country lost a man who would have made an excellent Taoiseach.

In 1968 Healy published his Death of an Irish Town (later No One Shouted Stop) which chronicled the rise and demise of his native Charlestown. Other books followed including Nineteen Acres in 1978 and Healy, Reporter in 1981. These works have symbolised the struggle of small towns in rural Ireland where the problems of a lack of critical size and a declining rural hinterland has seen their economies of scale contract while larger, more centralised locations drain the wealth and populations out from the smaller towns. Healy saw the development of Knock Airport in the 1980s as a ray of hope for the future especially in its ability to transform the local economy in County Mayo and in the west of Ireland generally.

John Healy's sudden death in 1991 at the age of 61 years robbed Mayo and Ireland of one of our foremost political commentators.

Monsignor James Horan

During his colourful lifetime, Monsignor James Horan (1911 – 1986) became one of the best-known priests in Ireland. Born near Partry, James Horan was educated at the local National School, St Jarlath's College, Tuam and St Patrick's College in Maynooth. Following his ordination, he worked for a few years in the Glasgow Diocese before returning to the Tuam Archdiocese and parish appointments in Galway and Mayo.

Fr Horan's entrepreneurial talents started to emerge during his tenure as a curate in Tooreen, near Ballyhaunis. He was responsible for the building of a large ballroom there that soon became a mecca for the leading showbands of the day and had a huge local following for young dance goers. It was in the pre-alcohol days of the early 1960s and 1970s where a joint visit by a couple to the 'mineral bar' became a barometer of how the budding romantic relationship was progressing.

Monsignor James Horan (Photo: IWAK/Mayo.IE)

Not all the local clergy or school teachers were overly impressed at the emergence of dance halls such as Tooreen and their perceived potential for young people to be led astray! Tales were told of young girls dancing in Tooreen Hall who suddenly noticed the cloven feet of their dance partner – surely the devil himself with nothing good on his mind... Nobody can recall any tales of young men noticing anything similar in their female partners! The dance hall boom ended in the mid-1970s and Tooreen Hall closed as a commercial venue.

Fr Horan became Parish Priest in Knock in 1967 after serving there for four years as a curate. One of his main contributions to Knock village was developing in conjunction with Mayo County Council an overall plan for the village and the building of a basilica in 1976. Much of the work went into providing facilities for pilgrims including a re-design of the Apparition Gable, hostels and better nursing care facilities for the sick and dis-abled as well as a museum and processional square. A key area in the development was the provision of improved parking facilities which had been a major headache for years especially during periods of bad weather.

The centenary of the 1879 Knock apparition was fast approaching in the years after his appointment and Fr Horan was fully tuned in to the opportunities this event offered. He convinced the Irish Hierarchy to invite Pope John Paul 11 as special guest for the 1979 celebrations. A visit to Knock Shrine was the chief goal of the Pope on his historic first papal visit to Ireland in 1979. Pope John Paul 11 attended Knock Shrine on the 30 September and was greeted by hundreds of thousands of fellow pilgrims. During his visit he confirmed Knock Church as a basilica and elevated Fr Horan to the rank of Monsignor.

After the papal visit, Monsignor Horan sets his sights on developing an international airport in east Mayo. His vision was two-fold – to provide better infrastructure in rural Ireland and to provide greater ease of access for pilgrims wishing to visit Knock Shrine. He used his excellent communication skills to convince local and national politicians as well as business that there was real merit in a centrally-located international airport in the middle of Ireland.

The first sod on the airport site 5 kms south of Charlestown was turned in May 1981 and though initial funding was often on a wing and a prayer, support for the project grew and the basic structures for an airport were gradually put into place. In October 1985, three Aer Lingus charter flights took off from Knock airport en route to Rome and signalled the de facto opening of the new facility. Monsignor Horan's dream of an international airport in his native Mayo had been realised.

He died suddenly on 1 August 1986 while on a pilgrimage to Lourdes and was buried in the grounds of Knock Basilica.

In 1984, Monsignor Horan had been named as Mayo Person of the Year. Few people deserved it more.

Dr. Kathleen Lynn (Photo: MAYO.IE)

Dr Kathleen Lynn

Dr Kathleen Lynn (1874 – 1955) was born near Killala and became one of the first Irish women doctors when she graduated in medicine in 1899 from the Royal University. She subsequently worked for ten years in the USA before returning to take up a position as the first female doctor at the Royal Eye and Ear Hospital.

Her career was notable for her devotion to the suffragette movement and her involvement in labour politics. James Connolly appointed her Chief Medical Officer of the Irish Citizen's army in 1913. She played a prominent part in the labour revolt and subsequent lockout of 1913-1914. The daughter of a Church of Ireland clergyman, she became even more committed to the Irish nationalist cause and was a very active medical officer in the 1916 Easter Rising. She became commanding officer of her own unit on the death of her superior, Sean Connolly.

After the suppression of the Rising, she was arrested and imprisoned in Kilmainham Jail where she remained till her release in 1917.

She was elected Honorary Vice President of the Irish Women's Workers' Union in 1917. The following year during the War of Independence she was arrested while on the run in South Tipperary. She was briefly imprisoned in Arbour Hill but a request from the Lord Mayor of Dublin secured her release to enable her to help with the Spanish Flu epidemic that was then ravaging Dublin.

In 1919, together with her lifelong partner, Madeleine Ffrench-Mullen, she established Ireland's first mother and child hospital, St Ultan's Hospital for Infants at 37 Charlemont St in Dublin. The hospital sought to provide much needed medical help and education to the poor and disadvantaged. Her research interests included tuberculosis and initial work on the emerging Bacille Calmette Guerin (BCG) vaccine.

On her death in 1955, the nursing staff of St Ultan's lined the route as the cortege passed her hospital. She was interred with full military honours in the family plot in Dean's Grange Cemetery. In 2016, Dr Kathleen Lynn was honoured with a commemorative stamp by An Post for her role in the Easter Rising a century earlier.

Stephen and Maureen Moore (Photo: Moore Family)

Stephen Moore

Stephen Moore is the most capped Australian rugby hooker of all time and captained Australia until his retirement from international rugby in 2017. During a stellar career in which he played for both Queensland Reds and the Brumbies in Super Rugby, Stephen amassed a total of 129 caps for his country. In 2015, he led Australia to the Rugby World Cup final only to lose to New Zealand.

Stephen has strong Mayo connections through his mother Maureen, nee Byrne, and grandparents, Martin and Bridget Byrne, née Kelly, from Kinaffe between Swinford and Bohola. The Byrne family moved to live in County Meath in the 1960s. Prior to being capped for Australia, Stephen's emerging talent attracted the interest of the IRFU but his rugby loyalties by that stage lay with his adopted country.

Stephen Moore has been a regular visitor to Ireland and Mayo down the years and has taken a keen interest in Mayo's All Ireland outings in recent years.

Mary Robinson

Mary Robinson was born Mary Bourke in Ballina in 1944, the only daughter of Aubrey and Tessa (nee O'Donnell) Bourke, who were both doctors. After an impressive law student career at Trinity College Dublin, the King's Inns and Harvard Law School, she became a barrister and progressed to become Reid Professor of Constitutional and Criminal Law at Trinity. Her legal career saw her involvement in high profile constitutional cases in Ireland, the

Mary Robinson (Photo: Nationaal comite 4 en 5 Mei)

European Court of Justice and the European Court of Human Rights. Her interest in politics progressed with election to Seanad Eireann as part of the Trinity College panel and she used this platform to further her interests in many social issues, women's rights, human rights and a more liberal approach to the law in Ireland.

Her election as President of Ireland in 1990 was unexpected at the start of the Presidential campaign but some notable slip-ups by the late Brian Lenihan (the Fianna Fail candidate) saw her campaign gain momentum. She was elected on transfers from the former Northern Ireland SDLP politician, Austin Currie, who was the official Fine Gael candidate.

Her election ushered in an era of outstanding Presidents of Ireland and a move away from the hard-core partisan politics that preceded her win.

Mary Robinson brought an immediate change to the office with an emphasis on social inclusion, the role of women – Mna na hEireann - the contributions of voluntary organisations in Irish society and a recognition of a role for the broader Irish diaspora throughout the world. Her symbolic light in the family kitchen at Aras an Uachtarain was a tangible recognition of those who had left their homes in Ireland to live abroad but were still a part of the Irish family.

In May 1933, President May Robinson visited her neighbouring Head of State, Queen Elizabeth 11 at Buckingham Palace in London. This historic visit represented the first meeting of the two Heads of State of the adjoining islands, Ireland and the United Kingdom, since the partitioning of Ireland and Irish independence in 1922. It represented major progress in Irish and UK relations and paved the way for a full state visit by President Michael D Higgins in April 2014.

Near the end of her seven-year stint as President of Ireland, Mary Robinson decided against seeking a second term in office and resigned in September 1997. She had been invited by the then United Nations Secretary General, Kofi Annan, to become the United Nations High Commissioner for Human Rights. In her subsequent memoirs, Mary Robinson expressed her regret at resigning her position as President of Ireland.

In 1998, she was made Chancellor of Trinity College Dublin and continued her interests in human rights and reconciliation. She donated an archive of her works and collections to the National University of Ireland Galway and Mayo County Council with the aim of establishing a formal centre in her native Ballina. Her family home, Victoria House, has been purchased by Mayo County Council and the aim is to establish a presidential library in her honour.

Michael and Ethna Viney

Michael and Ethna Viney are probably best known for their long-running, weekly column 'Another Life' published in the Irish Times since 1977. English-born Michael and his wife, Ethna, decided to forgo city life in Dublin and made their home south of Killadoon, under the shadow of Mwellrea mountain. The couple jointly wrote Ireland's Ocean: A Natural History.

Michael & Ethna Viney (Photo: M&E Viney)

Michael Viney has written numerous books on the flora and fauna of his adopted Mayo home but some of his most sought-after pearls of wisdom are found is his responses to readers' question in his weekly Another Life column. Ethna similarly contributes to The Irish Times column on a weekly basis and is a much respected environmental expert.

Dr T K Whitaker

Dr T K Whitaker is generally credited with being the brains behind the economic development of modern Ireland. He served with many governments of the day between his appointment as Secretary of the Department of Finance (1956 – 1969) and as Governor of the Central Bank of Ireland (1969 – 1976). He played a central role as economic advisor in Ireland's application to join the EEC (European Economic Community) in 1973.

Dr TK Whitaker (Photo: MAYO.IE)

He was universally respected across the political divide and on his retirement from the Civil Service in 1976, he served as a member of Seanad Eireann for two terms. He was appointed the first chairman of Bord na Gaeilge (1974 – 1978) and later as Chancellor of the National University of Ireland. He played a leading role in helping to forge enlightened, consensus politics towards ending the 'Troubles' in the North of Ireland. His influence was key to the Irish government adopting a policy on Ireland's claim to sovereignty over Northern Ireland based on consent of the people living there.

Whitaker loved fishing and in 1972 he bought a cottage in Gencullin, on the shores of Carrowmore Lake in Erris. He loved to return and stay in his Mayo hideaway and apart from his angling enjoyed mixing with the locals and using the Irish language. An excellent biography - T K Whitaker; Portrait of a Patriot – written by Mayo-born Anne Chambers, was published in 2014.

Section 5

Sport

Cora Staunton and Aidan O'Shea (Photo: Michael Donnelly)

MAYO GAELIC FOOTBALL LEGENDS

Mayo Team V Galway Connacht Final 1973 (Photo: Liam Lyons Collection)
Back: Joe Corcoran, Mick Higgins, Willie McGee, Frank Burns, John Morley, JP Kean, John Carey, John O'Mahony
Front: JJ Costello, Mick Begley, Sean Kilbride, John Gibbons, Tom Fitzgerald, Ger Feeney, Tommy O'Malley

1950 Mayo team that defeated Louth in the All-Ireland final
Back row: Dr Jimmy Laffey (Chairman Mayo GAA Board), Gerald Courell (trainer), John Forde, Henry Dixon, John McAndrew, Tom Langan, Joe Gilvarry, Tom Acton, Billy Durkin, Paddy Irwin, Sean Wynne, Mick Caulfield, Tommy Byrne, Sean Mulderrig, Eamonn Mongey, Paddy Prendegast.
Front Row: Jimmy Curran, Jackie Carney, Mick Flanagan, Peter Quinn, Sean Flanagan, Padraig Carney, Mick Mulderrig, Billy Kenny, Peter Solan, Mick Downey, (masseuse), Liam Hastings, Joe Staunton.

Dr M Loftus, Seamus O'Malley 1936 Capt and Dermot O'Brien, Louth winning Capt 1957 (Photo: Liam Lyons Collection)

Padraig Carney

They dubbed him the flying doctor, an epithet that stuck after flying him home from America for the league final of 1954. It was Padraig Carney's final game for Mayo. At 26, the end of a short, glistening football career.

Ten years earlier, as a 17-years-old, he made his senior debut for Mayo in a challenge against Galway, kicking a point with his first touch of the ball. The following year he was back in the minor team and winning a Connacht medal with the county. By the time a rejuvenated Mayo got to the All-Ireland final of 1948 Carney, at 20 years of age, was already a star on the national stage, having won Sigerson Cup medals with UCD two years in succession. In that year's Connacht final replay against Galway, Carney, playing at midfield, scored nine points.

Born in Treenagleragh, near Kiltimagh but reared in Swinford, the medical student was determined to make it to the top at Gaelic football. Self-motivated, he would spend hours alone practising free kicks, sprinting and running with the ball. As a young doctor in Castlebar he continued that regime, alone, in the grounds of St Mary's Hospital, kicking, kicking, kicking.

The 1948 All-Ireland final, his first, was to end in controversy. Fulltime was called by the referee with some three minutes of playing time remaining, and Mayo's Peter Quinn preparing to punch the ball over the bar for the equalising point. A minute earlier a close-in free-kick by Carney was illegally charged down by a Cavan player which went unpunished by the referee. Mayo had every right to feel hard done by.

But the blossoming of his career had yet to come. Two All-Irelands would follow, two National Leagues, four Connacht titles, and a couple of county senior medals won with Castlebar Mitchels while a doctor in the local hospital.

With a record of 11-198 in 55 league and championship appearances, Padraig is ranked seventh on Mayo's all-time scoring list, all that achieved more than sixty years ago.

Corcoran family - Joe Jnr, Mary, Joe and Catherina (Photo: Corcoran Family)

Joe Corcoran

The silence was eloquent. A lissom lad in motion held his audience breathless. Eyes pinned on the stripling as he chipped and turned and kicked and scored. All in perfect symmetry.

Words were superfluous. The scene in Ballina that summer evening was rich in reminiscence. Faint outlines of a Carney, a Mongey, a Flanagan in their heyday five years earlier flitted across the eyes of those who watched a hapless defence striving to curb this meandering menace.

Barely a teenager and unfamiliar with the rudiments of the game Joe Corcoran had burst onto the Mayo scene. There and then a new star was born, the brightest of the lot, with skills that were talked of long after the results of games were forgotten. The spoils of victory were few and far between for the Mayo that Joe Corcoran would eventually grace.

But the memories he left were of skills that would take your breath away. Memories of sinuous trails wound through defences, of skipped tackles, beautiful sidesteps and fine scores carved with left and right from all sorts of angles.

He won Connacht medals in 1967 and '69 and a National League in 1970. But few chances came his way to display his talents to a wider audience.

1951 All-Ireland winning Mayo team (Photo: Mayo.IE)

ck row l to R: James Quinn, Eugene Quinn (brothers of Fr Peter Quinn), Paddy Jordan, Mick Loftus, hn Forde, Joe Gilvarry, Tom Langan, Paddy Irwin, John McAndrew, Jimmy Laffey (chairman Mayo GAA Board), Henry Dixon, Liam Hastings, Mick Mulderrig, Gerald Courell (trainer), Pat Conway (treasurer). Front Row: Willie Casey, Jackie Carney (trainer), Sean Wynne, Mick Flanagan, Eamonn Mongey, Sean Mulderrig, Fr Peter Quinn, Padraig Carney, Sean Flanagan, Paddy Prendergast, Jimmy Curran, Joe Staunton.

Sean Flanagan

From across the road in Clonliffe College where he was a clerical student, Sean Flanagan could hear the thud of the ball in Croke Park. It was All-Ireland minor final day in 1940 and Mayo with whom he played up to the semi-final were fighting a losing battle with Louth without their key player . . .
because of college rules.

From there he went on to win five Connacht senior medals, lead Mayo to two All-Ireland titles, and captain Connacht to Railway Cup success in 1957. Of those successful teams, Flanagan at left corner back, and Tom Langan at full forward were accorded the distinction in 1984 of being selected by a panel of former players and journalists to the Gaelic Football team of the century. The selection was part of celebrations marking the centenary of the founding of the Gaelic Athletic Association.

Similarly, to commemorate the arrival of the new Millennium, a Gaelic football Team of the Millennium was chosen in 1999 by a panel of GAA past presidents and journalists. It was stipulated that those chosen should be in the same positions they held on their county teams. Flanagan and Langan of Mayo were duly chosen.

Joe Henry (Photo: Tooreen GAA Club)

Joe Henry

Hurling to Mayo is what football is to Kilkenny. Yet, one Mayo hurler stands tallest in Ireland. Joe Henry's 24 Mayo senior hurling medals – won with Tooreen – have not been equalled by any hurler in any part of the country.

Ciaran Dowds won his 24th with Burt of Donegal, and Limerick's famous Mackey brothers, Mick and John, have fifteen apiece won with Adare. But Joe Henry stands alone.

He won his first in 1972, and his last in 2000. In between is a history of enduring brilliance, the story of a man whose love of hurling flourished in the infertile hurling fields of Mayo . . . the story of triumph over adversity.

Joe also played Railway Cup hurling with Connacht, the only outsider on the all Galway side. And as if to prove that his skills were not confined to the small ball, the Tooreen man can also boast a Mayo senior football medal among his rich collection. It was won with Shamrocks in 1977, Joe coming from the bench in the second half and scoring the winning point . . . an hour after lining out with Tooreen in the Mayo senior hurling final.

Billy Kenny (Photo: Kenny Family)

Billy Kenny

Billy Kenny epitomised the spirit of the men of Mayo's golden era. His All-Ireland input ended fifteen minutes into the final of 1950, but his character was the inspiration for the back-to-back success of his colleagues.

As he was carried from the field in great pain with a compound fracture of a leg, the Claremorris native rose from the stretcher and lifted his clinched fist in a gesture all the rest of his team-mates fully understood. The gesture typified the whole outlook of Billy Kenny. All through his life in whatever had been his lot he had shown the same courage, the same determination, the same concern for others, and the same lack of consideration for himself.

Billy never played football again. He spent six months in hospital and six months convalescing. He qualified as a doctor – having given up a lucrative job with an oil company – married Kay Divilly from Headford and emigrated to Canada.

Billy built a brilliant reputation in Canada as a doctor, and in Burlington became one of its distinguished citizens. In 1958 he was the only citizen of the city (pop 50,000) listed in the Social Register of Canada. The following year he was elected president of the Lion's Club and named citizen of the year.

In 1959 five young boys in the city were burned in a fire. Billy Kenny was asked to tend them and his skills and expertise over a two-year period nursed the boys back to full health. He also organised the 'Burned Boys Fund' which raised $35,000.

He was involved, too, in the establishment of a new hospital in Burlington, brought in the first patient and presided over the first birth. His name became a household word around Burlington.

Later he contracted an illness that prevented him from practising as a doctor. In 1962 he came to Sligo with his wife and four daughters, then courageously hit for England to study, and was admitted a Fellow of the Institute of Dermatology at London University.

This great Mayo man returned to live with his family in Galway and worked at the Regional Hospital in the city for some time before he died.

Two trophies commemorating Dr Billy Kenny were presented for football competitions in Mayo: one, in 1971, was donated by Mayo GAA Board for his 'brave and spirited action'. The Kenny family donated another. Billy's daughter Dr Roseanne presented that trophy to the captain of its first winners, Pat Hyland of Shrule/Glencorrib.

Henry Kenny (Photo: Kenny family)

Henry Kenny

In an age when high fielding was critical to success Henry Kenny was an exemplar of the art. At midfield when Mayo were flying high in the 1930s Kenny was described as one of the most stylish midfielders of all time.

At the age of 17 he lined out with the Mayo senior side in 1931. He was a minor the following year also and on the senior side up to the All-Ireland-semi-final that same year. Because of his tender years he was omitted from the final against Kerry. But he remained a regular afterwards until he retired in 1946.

Honours: All-Ireland senior title; 6 National League medals; three Railway Cup and countless other medals.

Former Taoiseach Jack Lynch described Henry Kenny as a 'graceful colossus'. Roscommon's J.P. "Doc" Callaghan said there had never been anyone to equal Mayo's Henry Kenny and Paddy Kennedy of Kerry.

The Mayo 1936 All-Ireland team and officials pictured in New York in 1937.
Back, left to right: Paddy Mullaney, Bernie Durkin (Chairman), George Ormsby, Patsy Flannelly, Henry Kenny, Patrick Collins, Tom Burke, Paddy Quinn, Purty Kelly, Gerald Courell, Tom Grier, Tommy McNicholas, Séamus O'Malley. Front, left to right: Fr. Eddie O'Hara, Pat Brett, Jackie Carney, Jim 'Tot' McGowan, Paddy Moclair, 'Capt.' Paddy Munnelly, Peter Laffey, Billie Mongey, Josie Munnelly, Tommy Regan, John Clarke. Image from Terry Reilly's The Green Above The Red.

Mayo players en route to New York 1937 (Photo: Kenny family)
From left: Patsy Flannelly, Paddy Moclair, the captain of the ship, Henry Kenny and Purty Kelly as the Mayo team sailed to America in 1937.

Ciaran McDonald

On the pitch of Hong Kong football club in 2005 a group of GAA All-Stars watched as one player in practice went through the gamut of his skills. Ciaran McDonald had six or seven balls with him and was shooting from hands and ground from a variety of angles and distances.

Willie McGee in action (Photo: Liam Lyons Collection)

"He put spins on the ball, he put a bend on the shots, his accuracy sensational", said journalist Donal Keenan. "If we had thought to film it, it would have been an internet sensation. It was mesmerising stuff." Watching in awe were Peter Canavan, Declan Brown, Stevie McDonnell and "Gooch" Cooper.

McDonald scored seven points in Crossmolina's All-Ireland Club championship victory of 2001. He also helped Mayo to provincial Under 21 success and to Connacht senior titles in 1997, 1999 and 2003.

Willie McGee

Four-goal McGee. The epithet was coined following the four goals Willie McGee netted for Mayo in the All-Ireland Under 21 final replay against Kerry in 1967. The Burrishoole man scored many other fine goals for his county, none more spectacular than in the league final of 1972 against Kerry when his drop shot almost ripped the net from its rigging.

McGee was a member of the Mayo senior panel from 1967 until 1975 racking up of 29-35 with his educated left foot, a total that would have been much greater but for the injuries that kept him out of the game for long periods.

He was selected in 1984 at full-forward on the All-Ireland team of the century of players never to have won an All-Ireland senior title.

Ciaran McDonald, Supermac (Photo: Michael Donnelly)

John and Frances Morley and Joe Langan (Photo: Liam Lyons collection)

John Morley

Two weeks earlier John Morley was lying on his back in hospital having undergone an appendicectomy. Now the sterling defender is on the Croke Park sideline, straining at the leash for a chance to rescue Mayo's dwindling All-Ireland hopes.

The mentors give way to their zealous star, and you can almost feel the sting of the scar as he stretches for a ball. Mayo lose that semi-final to Meath in 1967, and Morley, around whose talent the team is built, was denied an All-Ireland final appearance.

He made a total of 112 appearances for his native county. In none did he give less than his best. And as a high fielder he was among the most graceful and effective in the country.

John Morley, a detective with the Garda Siochana, was killed on July 7, 1980, while pursuing burglars from a bank robbery in Ballaghaderreen.

Mayo 1936 All Ireland Team (Photo: Kenny family)

Back row (L-R): Paddy Moclair, Patsy Flannelly, Peter Laffey, Purty Kelly, Paddy Quinn, Paddy Brett, Tom Burke, Josie Munnelly, J.P. 'Tot' McGowan. Front (L-R); George Ormsby, Henry Kenny, Paddy 'Capt' Munnelly, Seamus O'Malley (Captain), Jackie Carney, Tommy 'Danno' Regan, Tommy Grier.

Josie Munnelly

Josie Munnelly won twelve county senior football medals with Castlebar Mitchels and one county hurling title. He was a member of Mayo's first All-Ireland winning senior side (1936) and at the age of 42 won an All-Ireland junior football medal with the county in 1957.

The character of the man can be gauged by his efforts to turn out for Castlebar Mitchels in a championship match in Westport. He was holidaying in his native Crossmolina at the time and set off from the North Mayo town to cycle the 21 miles to Castlebar.

At Pontoon a tyre burst, and the opportunity to meet up with the rest of the team seemed lost. Not to be bested, Josie carried the bike on his shoulders all the nine miles to St Mary's Hospital in Castlebar where he worked.

By then the team had left for Westport. So Josie togged out in the hospital while a colleague organised another bicycle. And with a topcoat over his playing gear he pedalled the ten miles to Westport reaching the playing ground sometime after the start of the game, but soon enough to play a major role in the Mitchels' win.

Some of the three All-Ireland winning Mayo teams at a match to celebrate the 30th anniversary of the 1936 All-Ireland victory.
Back row: Paddy 'Bluett' Graham, Gerald Courell, Dick Hearns, Henry Kenny, Todd Burke (son of goalkeeper Tom), Paddy Quinn, Paddy Munnelly, Sean Flanagan, Tommy Byrne, Eamonn Mongey, Willie Casey, Billy Mongey, J. Durkan, Tom Burke.
Front Row: John Joe McGowan, Jackie Carney, Jimmy Laffey, Paddy Moclair, Seamus O'Malley (capt '36 team), Jim 'Tot' McGowan, Tommy Grier, Tommy Regan, Josie Munnelly, Tommy Hoban, unidentified.

Paddy Prendergast Photo: (Mayo.IE)

Paddy Prendergast

No fullback in the history of the game has had greater distinction that Mayo's Paddy Prendergast of 1950-51 fame. No one in Ireland has surpassed the Ballintubber man's prowess in the No 3 jersey.

Not the tallest of fullbacks, yet with a cat-like spring that propelled him above most of his rivals to win possession with the safest of hands. He was regular fullback from 1948 to 1955 winning two All-Ireland, two national league and a host of other medals.

Padraic Carney, Orla and Dr Mick Loftus

Broadcaster Micheal O Muirceartaigh had this to say of Prendergast: "The most spectacular fullback ever . . . He claimed every ball that landed inside the '14'. He was wonderfully light-footed and was able to rise well to capture the high ball."

Mayo U21 v Kerry Sept 1973 Final Ennis (Photo: Liam Lyons Collection)

Back: Des McGrath, Con Moynihan, Ted Webb, S Langan, Ray McNicholas, J Culkin, S Reilly, J O'Mahony Front: P Cunningham, M Flannery, Eamonn Ralph, Ger Feeney, Ger Farragher, Richie Bell, M Gannon

Mayo team and subs on board the SS Manhattan sailing to New York in 1937.
Mayo team Back from left to right:
Seamus (James) O'Dwyer Ballyhanuis, John. J.Moran, Mick Moran Westport, Seamus O'Malley Ballinrobe, Jim Forde, Ballyhanuis, John Egan Castlebar, Tom Burke Castlebar, Patsy Flannelly Castlebar P.J. Purty Kelly Westport.

Middle Row from left:
Dr Sean Lavin Kiltmagh, Paddy Quinn Castlebar, John Clarke Ballina, Captain Karl Graalfs of SS New York Hamburg American Line, Bernie Durcan Bohola, Paddy Moclair Ballina, Dick Hearns Ballina.

Front Row from left:
Jack Kenny Westport, John Culkin Ballina, Gerard Courell Ballina, Michael Mulderrig Crossmolina, Patrick Munnelly (Known as Captain) brother of Josie Crossmolina and later Castlebar, Tom Tunney Charlestown and Ballaghaderreen Seamus Curran.

Current GAA Stars

Colm Boyle takes control (Photo: Michael Donnelly)

Colm Boyle

Colm Boyle from the Davitts club in South Mayo has been one of the most inspiring footballers of his generation. He originally started out as a wing half back but has seen stints in various locations including centre half back and sweeper. Invariably, when Mayo seem to be heading into troubled waters, Colm Boyle has been one of the key 'go-to' players in the team. It is a role he thrives on and, as befits the man, he invariably delivers the goods. His no-nonsense approach to his football has seen him occasionally on the receiving end of refereeing decisions. But his Mayo supporters love his tenacity and grit and what his inspirational play brings to the team.

He is the proud winner of five Connacht Senior Championship medals as well as four All Star awards.

Keith Higgins (Photo: Michael Donnelly)

Keith Higgins

Keith Higgins has played a stellar role in football and hurling both with his club Ballyhaunis and with Mayo. Renowned for his lightening acceleration, Keith initially started out as a left full back, then as a half back but has also enjoyed a spell as a sweeper and in the forwards. One of his hallmark plays involves a quick transition from the back to a scoring opportunity deep in the forward half of the pitch. His nickname 'Zippy' is very apt.

Keith has won seven Connacht senior football titles as well four All Star awards. Other notable achievements include Railway Cup medals with Connacht in hurling in 2007 and in football in 2014 – the first dual award winner from Connacht. He captained Mayo to Under 21 All Ireland success in football and won a Sigerson Cup medal in 2005. He was named Young Footballer of the Year in 2005.

Lee Keegan in action (Photo: Michael Donnelly)

Lee Keegan in full flight (Photo: Michael Donnelly)

Lee Keegan

His clashes with Dublin's Diarmuid Connolly have been the theme of football arguments whenever their names crop up. He admits to holding the Dublin man in the highest regard, but in their All-Ireland final epics, each has left nothing behind in his efforts to neutralise the effects of the other.

Lee Keegan has been the exemplar of a defensive philosophy with its roots in attacking football. From the halfback line his insight and vision have fashioned great scores for Mayo, his close marking tactics not endearing him to either opponents or referees. But in the four All-Star awards he has picked up, and the enviable honour bestowed on him as Footballer of the Year, lie the testimony of his rare qualities.

Asked once about his famous duels with Dublin's Diarmuid Connolly, the Westport man said it was his job as a defender to negate the influence of Connolly as much as possible.

"Believe me I love watching him play when he's in top form but I'm just there to do a job for Mayo and if I'm told to mark him that's just what I have to do.

"Maybe my name was being targeted for certain aspects of my game but I have no intention of stopping the hard way I play.

I play as fair as possible."

Forwards, he said, were recognised for their scoring ability and for setting up scores. Speaking up for his colleagues in defence, especially Keith Higgins and Colm Boyle who have also each won four All-Stars awards, the Westport man said: "We just look like the bullies and the thugs because we're the ones stopping them.

"Every supporter wants to see the forwards running around, kicking these beautiful scores and that, but we have to do the ugly work, the uncompromising stuff where we have to stop these players because if we don't there's no hope for us at all.

"As defenders you just have to do what other people are not willing to do. I've no beef with that at all. I'm very comfortable in saying that because I'm a defender and when it comes to winning games I have to stop a forward."

Keegan's All-Star awards were received in 2012, 2013, 2015 and 2016 the same year he was chosen Footballer of the Year. He has also won an Allianz League medal with Mayo in 2019 and an All-Ireland intermediate medal with his club Westport.

Andy Moran pivots (Photo: Michael Donnelly)

Andy Moran

Andy Moran has enjoyed an outstanding footballing career with Mayo culminating in winning the national 'Player of the Year' award in 2017. While All Ireland success at Senior level eluded him, the National League win in 2019 offered some consolation for a player generally regarded as a born leader amongst his peers.

Andy plays for the Ballaghaderreen club and has played over 160 times for Mayo. He tasted success on the Connacht Senior stage on eight occasions and won three Sigerson Cup medals. He won All-Star awards in both 2011 and 2017.

Cillian O'Connor strikes for goal (Photo: Michael Donnelly)

Cillian O'Connor

Cillian O'Connor assumed the role of Mayo's main free-taker in the Connacht final against Roscommon in 2011. He scooped eight points from frees in difficult conditions, guiding Mayo to their 43rd provincial crown. He was 19 years of age and it was his third senior championship game, the first in Ruislip when Mayo almost fell to London, the next against Galway, their closest rivals, before the final against Roscommon.

Born in 1992, he played with the county's minors in 2009 and captained the side the following year. He won a Connacht Colleges medal with St Gerald's College, Castlebar, beating Summerhill College, Sligo in the final. That same year, while still a minor, O'Connor helped his club Ballintubber to their first Mayo senior football title after which county manager James Horan called him into the senior squad.

He made his debut in a FBD league game in 2011, and his championship debut from the bench against London. For three years from 2013 he was football's top scorer in Ireland and won an All-Star award in 2014. In successive years he was chosen Young Player of the Year. And his leadership was recognised when appointed captain of the Mayo senior side.

Ever since, apart from time out with serious injury, Cillian O'Connor has been in the vanguard of Mayo's efforts to win their first senior All-Ireland title since 1951.

Diarmuid O'Connor (Photo: Michael Donnelly)

Diarmuid O'Connor

He was just 21 and those watching still talk about his inspired performance. It was an Allianz League clash in Clones in 2016 and Mayo had already been beaten by Dublin, Cork and Donegal. To remain in the premier division a win was vital. Their chances looked slim when Lee Keegan and Aidan O'Shea were dismissed during the game. It called for leadership and inventiveness. And it came from two men - captain for the day, Colm Boyle, and Diarmuid O'Connor.

In tandem with Boyle who led by example, tackling obsessively with no regard for his own safety, O'Connor, the youngest player on the field, also took the reins and assumed the quality of a star beyond his years. His work rate was extraordinary, his willingness to take on any task, tackle any opponent, to run himself to a standstill and bag a peach of a goal reaped an unlikely win that stood to Mayo for the remainder of the league.

Diarmuid O'Connor won an All-Ireland minor medal in 2013 while in Leaving Cert. A year later he was a member of the DCU Sigerson Cup wining side. He was among the goal scorers in his senior championship debut in 2014 against New York. That same year he received his first county senior medal with Ballintubber. Two years later he was on the All-Ireland winning Mayo under 21 team. And that same year was honoured with his second Young Footballer of the Year Award.

James Horan appointed Diarmuid captain of the Mayo senior team for 2019, the torch passing from his older brother, Cillian. It is an honour he will forever treasure. His first trophy acquired as captain was the winning of the Allianz League in 2019.

"I try not to think about the captaincy too much. This is a team full of leaders and to be honest it hasn't put any pressure on me," he said.

Aidan O'Shea in control (Photo: Michael Donnelly)

Aidan O'Shea sizes up the opposition (Photo: Michael Donnelly)

Aidan O'Shea

Aidan O'Shea is one of three brothers who lined out in the Connacht championship against Roscommon in 2014. He is in the middle, between Seamus and Conor, the first three Mayo siblings to be thus honoured. Aidan is most in the public eye, his performances the subject of more scrutiny than most. He's easy to find on the field. He's the big one, towering over everyone, out-fielding everyone, outplaying everyone.

He is also the target of more slings than most and has kept his nerve and dignity in the face of all sorts of provocation on and off the field. His strength and height are such that often only illegal challenges stop him, and many of those go unpunished.

It would seem the criticism of Aidan O'Shea has been for nothing more than just being himself, Aidan O'Shea, and the man all Mayo want him to continue being . . . the pillar of their county's performances.

The criticism of the Mayo star reached a climax when following a team talk after a match in Meath he broke from the group to sign autographs for admiring children. Watching was a former Meath footballer who said "that's exactly why Aidan O'Shea plays the way he does" implying he was not playing well, that in breaking from the group his discipline was in question, that he would prefer signing autographs than listening to what was being said.

It was a harsh observation of a player who like all players has had his off-days. The comment was condemned by the wider football public. His few off-days have generally been attributed to the position assigned to him, mostly at centre forward. His best performances have been at midfield where he has most room to exercise his array of talents.

His influence was sorely missed in the 2012 league campaign when out for some months with a serious injury. In the Connacht final he came from the bench to make an impact in Mayo's narrow win over Sligo.

O'Shea was a member of the Mayo team that reached the All-Ireland minor final in 2009, beaten by three points by Armagh. The same year he made his senior debut in the championship against New York and has been a crucial member in the cast of the Mayo journey since then.

His three All-Star awards attest to his stature. Interestingly each for a different position . . . midfield, full-forward and centre forward. His enormous contribution to Mayo football is not up for question. He has been the driving force of Mayo performances for many seasons. Long after he has retired the seminal accomplishments of the Breaffy man will be remembered.

Cora's a winner (Photo: Michael Donnelly)

Cora Staunton

The photograph was revealing. Lying in bed in a Sydney hospital, her broken leg in a cast, Cora Staunton bore the look of a person wondering had her celebrated career come to an end. Two seasons earlier at the age of 34 she joined the Western Sydney Giants, their first international signing. She had already decided on a further term, her third with the Australians, when she sustained the horrific injury in a club game against Macquarie University.

Cora was attracted to the Giants by her accomplishments as the outstanding ladies Gaelic footballer in Ireland. Her feats in the game over a period of 23 seasons are legendary, not least that at the age of 13 she lined out with Mayo. In that extraordinary career she won four senior All-Ireland medals with her native county and played in 68 championship games over 23 seasons.

At the age of 16 Cora led her club, Carnacon, to the first of six All-Ireland titles. She had trained as a juvenile with Ballintubber and was good enough to play alongside Alan Dillon, who became one of Mayo's greatest footballers.

They won numerous competitions as juveniles and she was accepted as 'just one of the lads'. She was playing with Carnacon at the age of eleven and scoring liberally against women double her age. That year too she won her first All-Ireland medal in Croke Park . . . the Primary Schools Girls Handball Championship.

Having broken her collarbone Cora was unable to line out with Mayo in the All-Ireland final of 1999. She was 17 and broken hearted. To ease her disappointment the Mayo manager allowed her take part in the pre-match parade in Croke Park, and to play for 45 seconds before being replaced. It was the first time the count-down clock was used for their games. Cora would later regret saying in the euphoria that followed Mayo's defeat of Cork in that final that they had done what the Mayo men failed to do. On that occasion team captain Diane O'Hora was the last to receive a cup before the old Hogan Stand was demolished in the refurbishment of Croke Park.

Cornacon followed up that win with three further successive All-Ireland senior titles, and Cora was one of their guiding lights. Fourteen years later, following their last All-Ireland, Mayo reached the final again, Cora still the heartbeat of the team. The lustre had not dimmed, but Mayo never emulated those early years of success. She also shared in Mayo's three National League titles.

Through the years Cora Staunton survived not only that broken collar bone but also a broken jaw, a broken nose, a serious knee injury and the death of her mother with whom she was very close. Nothing inhibited her passion for football or restricted her ability to carve out monstrous scores. She has survived intimidation on and off the field, cast it aside and refused to allow it to affect her game.

Having decided to join the Western Sydney Giants, Cora would travel to Clogher and in the fading light alone practice with the oval ball. She spent hours coming to terms with the capricious bounce of the ball. With other aspects of the Aussie game she felt at ease. And in her first match for the Australian club she adapted to the rules instantaneously and a new world had opened for this wonder woman of Mayo football.

The good news is that the Sydney injury did not end her career. Having recovered, Cora returned to her native county and was a member of the Carnacon team that won their 21st Mayo title in October 2019, twenty of them consecutively. Well done, Cora!

Mayo footballers Diarmuid O'Connor, Paddy Durcan, Lee Keegan and David Drake, Mayo Day 2019 (Photo: MAYO.IE)

Sporting rivalry and Mayo border towns

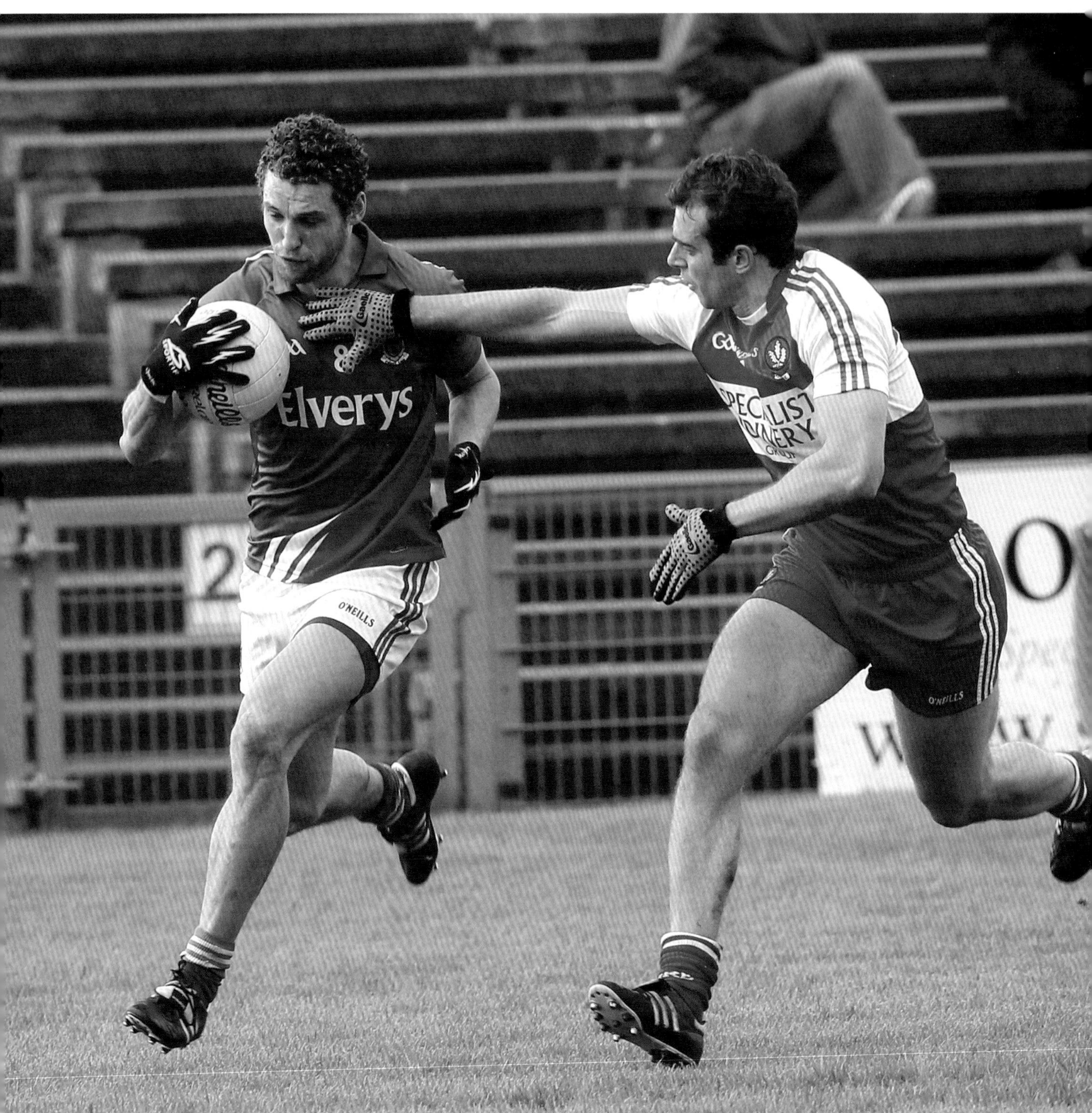

Tom Parsons cruises past (Photo: Michael Donnelly)

Border communities close to where Mayo joins Sligo to the north, Roscommon to the east and Galway to the south are well known for the intensity of their sporting rivalry and banter especially approaching senior championship matches during the Summer months. Whether it be in the local shops, at Mass, at weddings or funerals, loyalty to one's county somehow seems to acquire a certain steeliness as championship match days approach.

Public houses with large GAA followings such as Durkin's in Ballaghaderreen, Walsh's in Charlestown, Clarke's in Shrule and Gibbons's in Ballindine will all have one topic at the top of the conversation agenda 'How do you think we'll go on Sunday?', 'Can we do it this year?', or, at times, 'Have we any hope at all?'

Charlestown, one of the border towns in Mayo, straddles Sligo to the north at Bellaghy and is close to Ballaghaderreen in County Roscommon to the east. 'Ballagh' still plays its football in Mayo for historical reasons as it was part of the re-alignment of the Barony of Costello in 1898 when part of the parish of Kilbeagh together with Kilcolman and Castlemore were ceded to Roscommon as part of the Local Government (Ireland) Act.

Founded in 1888, Charlestown Sarsfields won its first Mayo Senior Football title in 1902 but had to wait another 99 years to win its second in 2001, followed by a third in 2009. A significant feature of many Mayo clubs has been the feature of multiple members of the same family featuring in the same team. For Charlestown, the Walshs, Tunneys, Swords, Bretts, Kearneys, Collerans, Henrys, Caseys and Higgins families have been stalwarts down the years. In the 1970s, three Kearneys, three Henrys and four Bretts were regulars for Charlestown and sometimes comprised two-thirds of the starting fifteen!

Eamonn Walsh captained Mayo minors to All-Ireland glory in 1953 and played regularly for Charlestown and Mayo in the succeeding years. His brother, the indomitable Frank, captained a losing 1947 Mayo minor team. Tommy (Danno) Regan held the right half back position on the All Ireland winning team of 1936. Notably, he maintained a Charlestown stranglehold on the Mayo right half position that began with fellow clubmen Fred Doherty (1917-1926), Tom Tunney (1926-1934) and continued by Danno from 1934 until 1944 – a staggering 27 years with no other club getting a look in!

Dr Padraig Carney worked for a year as dispensary doctor in Charlestown in 1953 and played with the Sarsfields that year to win a Mayo Junior Championship medal before emigrating to pursue his medical career in the United States. He was only 26 years old and still to reach his prime…

The success of the 2001 and 2009 Charlestown teams was built around the steely backbone provided by David Tiernan, Aidan Higgins and John Casey as well as a well organised club structure including under age teams. The Celtic Tiger helped too with local work opportunities ensuring key players no longer emigrated for Summer employment overseas.

The 2009 victory saw the emergence of 20 Year Tom Parsons as a rising star of the game. His significant knee injury in the Connacht Championship match against Galway in 2018 put his playing career on hold. Thankfully, after a long period of treatment and rehabilitation which showed his dedication and fortitude to return to the top flight, Tom made a cameo appearance off the bench in Mayo's loss to Dublin in the All Ireland Semi-Final in August 2019. Of course, Tom himself is a Sligo man from across the border in Bellaghy!

Some of Ballaghaderreen's footballing elite include Sean Flanagan who captained Mayo to All Ireland glory in 1950 and 1951. His son, Dermot, occupied his father's left full back position, also captained Mayo, as well as winning All-Star recognition in the process. Sean Kilbride played for both Mayo and Roscommon in the 1970s and 1980s while the sporting O'Mahony family provided three members to Mayo's underage and senior teams with John seeing All Ireland success with Galway as Team Manager.

Andy Moran arrives on the scene (Photo: Michael Donnelly)

Andy Moran has been one of the great stalwarts of the Ballaghaderreen team for many years. He captained Mayo as well as winning Connacht and National League honours plus All Star awards and Player of the Year in 2017. Other famous stars included John Morley, Con Moynihan and Frank Burns and they all had a penchant for the centre half back shirt!

The village of Shrule is separated from Galway by the Black River to its south. The locality around Shrule Castle, built by the Norman de Burgo family in 1238, has been the scene of many epic and brutal battles including the Battle of Shrule in 1570 between the Galway-based Clanrickarde Burkes and the Mayo MacWilliam Burkes.

Another massacre occurred in 1642 in the aftermath of the 1641 rebellion and subsequent Cromwellian invasion when up to a hundred plantar refugees fleeing to Galway were put to death. The local football banter and rivalry between modern day Shrule and its closest Galway neighbour, Caherlistrane, can be intense at times but is never that bad....

Shrule Glencorrib reached the final of the Mayo Senior Championship in 2005 but lost to Crossmolina in the final. As with many clubs, a footballing set of brothers, the Mortimers, had a powerful impact on the club's rise to prominence. Kenneth won GAA All Star awards in both 1996 and 1997 as a right corner back. Two other brothers, Trevor and Conor, along with Mark Ronaldson provided much of the sparkle in their glory years.

Conor won an All-Star award as right corner forward on the 2006 team. He played on losing Mayo teams in both 2004 and 2006 when Kerry were victorious. He was top scorer with 1 goal and 32 points in the 2006 All Ireland series. He also played for Connacht in the Railway Cup and later in his career with the Parnells GAA club in Dublin.

The amalgamation of close neighbours Ballindine and Irishtown GAA clubs to form Davitts GAA club occurred in 1974. The new club's name honours the historical legacy of Michael Davitt of Land League fame and the famous meeting he helped organise in Irishtown in April 1879 with up to 20,000 attending. Michael Davitt was also a founding patron of the GAA in 1884.

The Davitts club grounds are located just north of the Mayo – Galway border in Ballindine along the N17 road between Claremorris and Tuam. In 2011, Davitts won the Mayo and Connacht Intermediate Club football championship and finished runner-up in the All Ireland final in the Spring of 2012.

Colm Boyle is Davitts most recognised and decorated player. He has always been known for his great tenacity, speed and work rate and these features have contributed on many occasions when Mayo desperately needed a rallying force in some of their games. His career highlights include four All Star awards, Connacht championship success on five occasions as well as the heartbreak of four All Ireland defeats. He was also honoured with selection for Ireland in the International Rules series versus Australia in 2013 and 2014.

His Davitts colleague Michael Conroy has also seen success with seven Connacht senior titles with Mayo as well as featuring in the losing All Ireland Final against Donegal in 2012.

One of the remarkable success stories of Mayo GAA has been that of the Garrymore GAA club. Founded in 1918, the club rose to prominence in the 1970s and 1980s notching up six Mayo Senior Championship titles between 1974 and 1982. It won the Connacht Club Championship title in 1981 only to fall to Nemo Rangers in the All Ireland Final in the spring of 1982. Stalwarts of the club in their most successful era included Vincent Nally, TJ and Ger Farragher, Danny Dolan, Billy Fitzpatrick and more recently Enda Varley and Shane Nally.

Garrymore is very much a rural club situated close to the Mayo – Galway border and draws its players from an area roughly between Crossboyne, Roundfort and Milltown. Three in a row Galway All Ireland winner Noel Tierney played with Garrymore in his youth before John 'Tull' Dunne drafted him into the Galway set-up and the rest is history. Sometimes these borders work in your favour and sometimes not…

Kilmaine in south Mayo is close to the Galway and boasts footballing heroes in Des and Joe McGrath while elder brother PJ excelled at refereeing. Further north, Ballyhaunis, Aghamore, Kilkelly and Kilmovee lie close to the Roscommon border. Apart from modern day hero, Keith Higgins, Ballyhaunis also produced the GAA equivalent of soccer's Ronaldo in the 1970s with excitement machine Ted Webb. Sadly, Ted died all too young but his short sporting career brought some great memories for those of us lucky enough to have seen him play.

Aghamore, Kilkelly and Kilmovee areas have produced many GAA stars down the years including Sean Freyne in the 50s, Sean O'Grady and Jimmy Burke in the 70s while modern day heroes include Brendan Harrison, Fergal Boland and Alan Freeman.

In the Connacht final of July 1975 played in Sligo, eight of the starting Mayo team played their football with 'border' clubs!

Mayo V Sligo 1975 Connacht Final Sligo (Photo: Liam Lyons Collection)

Back: Eamonn Brett, Ted Webb, Ivan Heffernan, Con Moynihan, Frank Burns, TJ Farragher, Willie McGee, J O'Mahony Front: Mick Higgins, Ger Farragher Sean Kilbride, Tommy O'Malley, JP Kean, Ger Feeney, S Reilly

TOM LANGAN, RONAN O'GARA - MAYO CONNECTIONS

Tom Langan stamp (Photo: An Post)

Tom Langan, Mayo GAA star of the forties and fifties, and Ireland rugby legend Ronan O'Gara, have a common Mayo connection. Ballina born Joan O'Gara (nee Langan), mother of Ronan, is a cousin of the great Mayo full-forward. Both men reached the pinnacle of their respective sports, Langan bestowed with every honour in Gaelic football, O'Gara every conceivable rugby distinction with Munster, Ireland, the British and Irish Lions and world rugby.

A native of Ballycastle, Tom Langan won a Mayo Senior Gaelic Football Championship with his home club while still a minor. He debuted for the Mayo senior team in 1943 and played centre-half forward in the team that lost the 1948 All-Ireland Final to Cavan by a solitary point. Things got better for Tom in this golden era of Mayo football and he won two successive All-Ireland medals with Mayo in 1950 and 1951 while playing at full forward. He announced his dominance of the full forward position by scoring two goals in the semi-final win over Armagh and followed that up with an equally impressive display in the defeat of Louth in the final in September 1950.

His display in the 1951 All Ireland semi-final has reached legendary proportions. Mayo appeared headed for almost certain defeat with Langan playing at left half forward against a Kerry team under the stewardship of the famous Paddy Bawn Brosnan, holding on desperately to their lead. A tactical switch saw Langan moved to full forward and before Paddy Bawn had time to size up his new opponent, the man from Ballycastle launched his frame goalwards, swivelled in mid-air before punching the ball into the back of the Kerry net. Mayo escaped with a draw. Paddy Bawn had met his match. Mayo won the replay and in the final Tom Langan stamped his authority on proceedings by scoring a vital goal as Mayo ran out worthy winners over Meath by five points. Sam Maguire was back in Mayo for the second year in succession.

Tom Langan won two National League medals and five Connacht titles with Mayo as well as two Railway Cup medals with Connacht. He retired from the game following the 1956 Connacht final defeat to Galway. He continued his working career with the Garda Siochana (Irish Police Force) which he joined in 1944. He was mainly attached to the Bridewell station in Dublin and progressed to the level of Garda Detective. During his time in Dublin, he was a well-respected police officer and was a good friend of a founding member of the Dubliners – Luke Kelly. He died in 1974 just short of his 53rd birthday. Ten years later, fellow Mayo man and President-elect of the GAA, Dr Mickey Loftus from Crossmolina, opened the Tom Langan GAA Park in his native Ballycastle dedicated in his honour.

Tom Langan's cousin, Michael, lived in Ballina and together with his wife, Marion, produced a family of seven, the third eldest of five daughters being Joan Langan. After an undergraduate career at University College Galway where she also featured prominently for the College's camogie team, Joan teamed up with the fast and exciting UCG and Connacht rugby winger, Fergal O'Gara, a native of Ballisodare, Co Sligo. Romance led to wedding bells and the couple headed off to San Diego in California where Fergal had secured a post-graduate position in Microbiology. Their first son, Ronan John Ross O'Gara, was born in Sacramento in March 1977. The O'Garas returned to Cork later that year with Fergal becoming Professor of Microbiology at UCC and Joan resuming her teaching career.

Ronan O'Gara came under the radar of teacher and rugby coach, Declan Kidney while a student at Presentation Brothers College in Cork and this relationship was critical in his rugby development. At UCC, Ronan won an All-Ireland Under 20s medal before later switching to Cork Constitution. The era of professional rugby union had arrived and Irish rugby, especially Munster rugby, was quick to grasp the potential that was being offered.

Ronan was first capped by Munster as a 20-year-old in 1997 and went on to make 240 appearances for the province amassing 2,625 points along the way until retiring in 2013. He became the epitome of the professional rugby player with consistent performances many of which were match winning ones under severe pressure. Munster won Heineken Cups in 2006 and 2008 with O'Gara the master tactician. He was awarded the ERC European Player Award in 2010 to honour the player regarded as making the greatest contribution to rugby in the first 15 years of the Heineken Cup.

His Irish career was just as emphatic. After making his debut in 2000, Ronan went on to make 128 appearances for Ireland scoring 1,083 points in the process. He was an integral part of the Irish side that won the Triple Crown and Championship in 2006. He scored all of Ireland's points in the Triple Crown decider against Scotland at Murrayfield in 2007. His drop goal in the 78th minute proved to be the decisive score.

When rugby was played in Croke Park for the first time in 2009, Ronan had the honour of scoring the first international try there. He toured Australia, New Zealand and South Africa in 2001, 2005 and 2009 with the British and Irish Lions, gaining two caps along the way. After retiring in May 2013, Ronan undertook a four-year defence coaching role in Paris with Racing 92 before re-locating to Christchurch Crusaders as Assistant Coach in 2018. He moved to La Rochelle in France in July 2019 as head coach.

Another interesting but non-genetic sporting link between the O'Garas and the Langans and their Mayo connections is that their Ballina roots are held in common with other Irish capped rugby players. Gavin Duffy is a Ballina local while Fergus McFadden has a Ballina mother, one of the rugby-playing Lowry clan. Remarkably they all hail from the same Bohernasup suburb. The environment must be conducive.

Ronan and Joan O'Gara (Photo: O'Gara Family)

Joan and Fergal O'Gara (Photo: Tom Brett)

SOCCER IN MAYO

Castlebar Celtic club

Soccer in Mayo is organised through the Mayo Association Football League (Mayo AFL) which was originally founded back in 1954 with Westport Town, Castlebar Celtic, Barcastle and Quay Hearts the four founding members. Over the years, both Westport United and Castlebar Celtic have been the most successful teams in the league with the latter emerging victorious in the first season. In the 1970s, interest in soccer expanded and three different divisions were established. The top division is now known as the Elverys Sports Super League and is ranked at level seven in the Republic of Ireland football league system. Ballina Town emerged as champions in 2018 with Castlebar Celtic victorious in 2019.

Westport United was originally formed in 1911 and have won the Mayo AFL for a record 21 times. They have a long association with Bohemians FC in Dublin and the two clubs share the same red and black colours. The Westport team's official name has altered between Westport Town and Westport United over the years with United the current preferred name. In the 2004-2005 season, Westport United won the FAI Junior Cup, the only Mayo soccer club to win this coveted trophy.

Castlebar Celtic was founded in 1924 and they too share colours with a more prominent Scottish team – Glasgow Celtic. Castlebar were Mayo AFL champions for five years in a row between 1957-58 and 1961-62. They repeated the feat in the period between 1980 – 81 and 1986 – 87. They moved to their current ground at Celtic Park with the establishment of the Mayo AFL in 1954. Overall, they have been Mayo AFL champions on 10 occasions and finished as runners-up on 14 occasions.

Ballina Town was founded in 1961 and they were originally known as St Patrick's FC before switching to their current name after six months. They play their home games at Belleek Park and wear a white and blue strip. Their first of five victories in the Mayo AFL came in 1988-89 season and they have been runners-up on a further seven occasions.

Other current Super League teams who have won the league's top competition include Manulla FC (4 occasions), Straide and Foxford (3 occasions) as well as Ballyglass (3 occasions). Current Super League clubs still trying to reach the pinnacle include Ballyheane AFC, Charlestown Athletic, Erris United and Conn Rangers. Other notable winners no longer in the top flight include the indomitable, fairy tale winners Urlaur (1989-90 and 1991-92), Balla and Sporting

Westport (2 each) as well as Achill Rovers, Quay Hearts and Westport Crusaders with one win each.

Tom Ketterick, a founder member of Castlebar Celtic Football Club in 1924, was one of the great soccer personalities in Mayo. For his devotion to soccer, Tom suffered the taunts of some Gaelic games' stalwarts during the club's formative years.

Tom Ketterick Castlebar Celtic (Photo: PRO Castlebar Celtic)

Following the death of his wife in 1971 and at the age of 52, Tom moved to Ballina to live with his daughter and her family. But Castlebar was the font of his most cherished memories. He remained deeply involved with Celtic and saw it progress to be one of the leading soccer clubs in Mayo.

He tried playing Gaelic football at an early age but was too light and 'used to get murdered'. Hence, his decision to take up soccer where he soon became absorbed. He would gather the lads living around New Antrim Street, Tucker Street, Lucan Street, Knockthomas and Barrack Bridge, and they played a group from Higher ends of the town every other day, on the Mall.

Seamie Daly, a Gaelic games stalwart played with the Higher Ends 'against the wishes of his father who was very pro GAA,' as Tom put it. "We were in the trucking business doing some work for the County Council and each time I called to the offices I was referred to as the Englishman. It was the type of derogatory remark I had to put up with all my life because of my involvement with soccer."

His friend Joe Kilroy was a great soccer and Gaelic player. Joe played minor football for Mayo and was a member of the team which won a Connacht Minor title in the Thirties. "They reached the All-Ireland final," said Tom, "but Joe never got his Connacht medal because he played soccer."

When he started promoting soccer, Tom and John Burke, brother of Mayo goalkeeper Tom Burke of the 1936 All-Ireland winning side, were the only ones playing. Because they couldn't get a team together in Castlebar, they cycled from their homes to play with Quay Hearts in Westport.

Tom's connections with Westport were through his first cousins, the Kettericks, who lived in Peter Street. Pat was the father, Tommy and Martin the sons, and there were several girls including Kathleen. Tom's grandparents lived in Cahernalurgan where he played football.

Tom Ketterick was also a life-long supporter of Sligo Rovers and often travelled from Ballina to Sligo for home matches. He died at the age of 99 in 2013.

Rugby in Mayo

Westport RFC grounds Carrowholly (Photo: Daphne Haire)

Westport Rugby Football Club which was founded in 1925 is Mayo's oldest club and one of the oldest in Connacht. Known as The Bulls, Westport RFC formerly played their games at the Demesne in the grounds of Westport House before purchasing land in Carrowholly on the Golf Course Road. The new pitches and club-house were officially opened in 1986. The club currently fields two teams in Connacht Junior Leagues as well as well as under age teams and minis.

Stephen Walsh was Club President for many years and was also President of the Connacht Branch IRFU. Current President is Joe Grady.

Stephen Walsh (Photo: Westport RFC)

Sean Murphy turns first sod on Ballina RFC new grounds, (Photo: Gerry O'Donnell)

Ballina RFC, known as the Sea-Horses, currently plays in Division 2C of the All-Ireland League and has its home ground at Heffernan Park, on Creggs Road. The club was founded in 1928 and Martin Boland is the current club president. Down the years Ballina RFC have produced some outstanding ambassadors for the game – none more so than the legendary Sean Murphy a long-term Club President and a former President of Connacht Branch IRFU. His son, Peter, has taken up the mantle and has also served as Connacht Branch President.

In recent times, Ballina man, Gavin Duffy, has played rugby for Ireland and Connacht. Mick Moylette, from Ballina and Michael Sherry from Foxord were capped for Ireland in the 1970s while David Heffernan has represented Ireland and is currently playing with Connacht. Caelan Doris from Lacken is the newest Mayo and former Ballina player to be capped for Ireland making his debut against Scotland in February 2020. Other Ballina RFC stalwarts over the years include Aubrey and Oliver Bourke, Liam Molloy as well as Gerry O'Donnell, Michael Rowe, Tommy Cooke and Seamus O'Dowd.

Castlebar RFC was also founded in 1926 but only became affiliated with the Connacht Branch in 1934. The club grounds are at Clondreash and Johnny McCormack is the current club president. In recent years, the club has invested heavily in under teams with strong representation at Under 17s, Under 15s, Under 13s and minis. The club plays in the Connacht Junior 1C League but also feature in the Connacht Junior Cup and the Cawley Cup. In 2020, Castlebar and Connemara reached the final of the Connacht Junior Cup. Due to the COVID-19 pandemic, the final was not played and Castlebar and Connemara were declared joint winners.

Ballinrobe RFC and Ballyhaunis RFC are the two remaining rugby clubs in Mayo. Ballinrobe play their home matches at The Green and are represented in Connacht Junior Leagues as well as having under age teams. Ballyhaunis was formed in 1977 with Dr Alan Delaney one of the driving forces behind the team in the 1970s and 80s. On St Stephen's Day 1979, Ballyhaunis played a friendly fixture against rugby players from Charlestown with the match ending in a draw. Sean and Kitty Walsh provided the pitch for the match as well as contributing in no small way to the hospitality afterwards!

Paddy Beatty presents Connacht Cup to Tommy Cooke (Photo: Gerry O'Donnell)

GOLF IN MAYO

As befits a county with a large coastline and a hinterland displaying some of the most picturesque vistas to be found anywhere on the island of Ireland, Mayo possesses its quota of international standard golf courses and clubhouses. To satisfy the golfing needs of visitor and native alike, Mayo has seven 18-hole courses spread throughout the county while there are also some excellent nine-hole courses, often in prime locations.

9th Westport GC

Westport GC

15th Westport GC

15th Westport GC

Westport Golf Club, which was initially founded in 1908, moved to Carrowholly in 1915. A major re-vamp of the design and drainage system of the course was undertaken by Fred Hawtree and his team with the new course opening in 1975.

Westport has hosted the Irish Close Championship on four occasions with many famous golfers making their names there – notably the 15-year-old amateur Rory McIlroy - who won in 2005. Three years earlier in 2002, Paul McGinley set the course alight with a course record 65 on his way to winning the Smurfit PGA Championship. In 2008, the golfing Maguire sisters fought out the final of the Lancome Irish Ladies Close Championship with Lena overcoming Lisa.

The course has numerous stunning backdrops with Croagh Patrick, Clew Bay and Clare Island never failing to deliver the feel-good factor by simply being there. On the back nine, holes 11 to 15 are especially memorable.

Carne GC (Photo: Mayo.ie)

Carne Golf Club near Belmullet is another top quality 18-hole course set in a natural environment on the Mullet Peninsula that required minimal ground-works to enhance its dramatic appeal. The location was developed by Erris Tourism starting in 1992 with the opening of the front nine and followed three years later with the opening of the clubhouse in 1995. Its development coincided with the opening of Ireland West Airport at Knock and this international facility has been the port of entry for many golfers and visitors to this unique part of County Mayo.

Carne is regarded as being among the Top 10 golf courses in Ireland and among the Top 50 in Britain and Ireland. It is a must visit for all golfers but probably best played for the first time on a nice sunny Summer's day! It will draw you back.

Ballinrobe Golf Club originally opened in 1896 but this was replaced by a high quality, Eddie Hackett-designed, 18-hole golf course that was opened in 1995. The new international standard course was constructed on the Cloonacastle Estate, a few kilometres outside the town of Ballinrobe on the road to Claremorris. It has some exciting holes with the Par 4 tenth hole featuring a tee adjacent to the historic castle and finishes with a deceptive island green that soon sorts out your knowledge of distance and your choice of club.

The Ballinrobe course has been ranked Best Parkland Course in Connacht in both 2011 and 2013. Padraig Harrington considers it the best parkland course in Ireland and is a big fan of the Par 3s as well as the fifth hole that takes advantage of the natural landscape formed by the River Robe. Ballinrobe is a good test for the average standard golfer and it certainly pays dividends if you keep straight and out of the thick rough.

Castlebar Golf Club is another 18-hole, parkland golf course adjacent to Castlebar that has undergone extensive re-development in recent times. It has some testing Par 4s and Par 5s that provide a stern test of skill for any golfer.

Claremorris Golf Club is located between Claremorris and Ballindine on the N17. It too has undergone some major developments in recent years with drainage now much improved. It is a parkland course that is adjacent to the River Robe for some holes.

Club House Ballinrobe GC

13th Ballinrobe GC

Club House Castlebar Golf Club

Castlebar 16th

Ballina Golf Club is located on the Ardnaree side of Ballina and offers a good 18-hole test of your golfing ability. In former years, the doyen of Mayo football, Joe Corcoran, perfected his skills as a top-quality scratch golfer around the course and brought many national and provincial honours to the club.

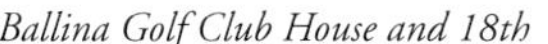

Ballina Golf Club House and 18th

Ballina Golf Club 1st facing Ox Mountains

Mulranny Golf Club, which was first founded in 1896, is a prime example of the perfect location to establish a golf course. The 5729 metre, 2 x 9-hole course has many outstanding vistas with Clew Bay lapping at its edges while Croagh Patrick, Clare and Achill Islands providing opportunities for conversation and visual appreciation of County Mayo's natural grandeur at almost every turn.

Mulranny Golf Club (Photo: Oliver Whyte)

Ballyhaunis GC

Ballyhaunis, Swinford, Achill and Ashford Castle all feature top quality nine-hole golf courses that possess their own natural beauty as well as tests of golfing ability. Access for a game is generally much easier at these 9-holers compared with the 18-hole courses and you can be certain of a warm welcome or an invitation to join a 3-ball or 4-ball if travelling alone.

Doohooma has a very picturesque 18-hole Par 3 golf course that the locals are always willing to share – whether visitors or Mayo natives alike. It is well worth a visit on your next trip to North-West Mayo.

HORSE RACING IN MAYO

Racing at Ballinrobe (Photo: MAYO.IE)

Ballinrobe racecourse, located just north of the town on the Castlebar road, is the only racecourse in Mayo and one of just four currently operating in Connacht – the others being Galway, Sligo and Roscommon. Ballinrobe is a popular course and was named Racecourse of the Year in Ireland in 2012. It has been at its current location since 1921. The course prides itself on its scenic outlook and excellent viewing facilities.

The castle located within the right-handed circuit with the Partry Hills in the distance adds to the charm of the location. Ballinrobe currently holds nine race meetings a year – seven national hunt and two confined to flat racing.

In 1993, Doran's Pride won his maiden race at Ballinrobe and progressed to win the Stayers' Hurdle at the Cheltenham festival in 1995. He subsequently won the Kerry National and Powers Gold Cup in 1997 followed by the Henessey Cognac Gold Cup in 1998. From his bumper win at Ballinrobe, his career earnings amounted to over 657,000 pounds sterling.

There has long been a tradition of beach racing in County Mayo with families and visitors drawn to the spectacle during the Summer months. Beach racing was held for many years at Carrowmore Beach near Louisburg before later moving to Cross near Killeen and to Killadoon Beach where they were last held in 1982. Since 2019, the **beach racing** festival has been successfully staged at Carrowniskey Beach and continues to prove very popular.

Joe and Anne-Marie McGowan with Davy Lad (Photo: JBMcG)

In North Mayo, the Doolough beach races are held a few miles outside Geesala and are strongly promoted as a very family friendly event. North of Killala, the Lacken Strand races are held during the month of May.

Mayo owners have been associated with racing at various levels down the years. Charlestown native, Joe McGowan achieved the ultimate prize in National Hunt racing by taking the Blue Riband Cheltenham Gold Cup with **Davy Lad** in 1977. Ridden by Dessie Hughes in the colours of Anne-Marie McGowan and trained by Mick O'Toole, Davy Lad started about fourth favourite in the race.

As his more highly fancied opponents including Lanzarote and Bannow Rambler fell and exited the race, Davy Lad found himself the highest backed horse still standing over the final few fences. He overtook the Tommy Carberry mount, Tied Cottage and Sommerville in the last few furlongs to ride out to a famous victory at 14/1. It is reported that Mick O'Toole had accepted a 50/1 offer on such a win four months earlier and was not disappointed. The 350,000 pounds sterling first place prize wasn't bad either.

Davy Lad had shown early signs of his future competence two years earlier with victory in the Sun Alliance Novice Hurdle at Cheltenham in 1975. The O'Toole stable repeated the feat with the McGowan-owned Parkhill victorious in the same event in 1976.

Back in the 1800s, the owners of Westport House had a keen interest in breeding thoroughbreds and one of their horses, **Waxy Pope** (or Lord Sligo's Waxy) won the English Derby in 1809. Howe Peter Browne became Lord Sligo after the death of his father in 1809 and bred horses at both the Curragh and at Westport.

It is interesting to note that the two biggest events in National Hunt and flat racing in Britain and Ireland have both been won by individuals with strong Mayo connections. Neither could be accused of lacking flamboyance or ambition.

Davy Lad 1977 (Photo: JB McGowan)

SECTION 6

MUSIC, SONG AND MAYO'S DARK SKIES

Letterkeen Bothy (Photo: Brian Wilson)

MISE RAIFTEIRI, AN FILE

Every Mayo schoolchild has learned to recite the poems of Anthony Raftery (Antoine O'Raifteiri) during their formative, primary school days. When it came to the opening verse of Raftery's signature poem – Cill Aodhain - the delivery usually contained some extra gusto with the line 'Go seasfaidh me sios i lar Chontae Mhaigh Eo.'

Raftery was born in Killedan (Cill Aodhain) between Kiltimagh and Bohola in 1779. He was one of nine children but sadly eight of his siblings tragically died from smallpox over a three-week period. Poor Anthony himself was left blind (suile gan solas) due to the smallpox and it is reported that his last memory of his siblings was of eight dead bodies laid out on the floor of their home.

Raftery's father was a weaver who worked mainly for a local landlord, Frank Taaffe. Because of his visual handicap, Anthony made a living playing the fiddle as well as reciting his poems and singing songs as a wandering minstrel in the local big houses of the better off. Raftery fell out with Taaffe after an accident in which one of his landlord's prize horses was killed. Because of the accident, Raftery got banished from the household and he subsequently became an itinerant poet/wandering bard spending most of the rest of his life travelling the roads of counties Mayo and Galway. He was a well-respected poet but the significance of much of his work only became well known in later years.

He died in Craughwell, County Galway in 1835 and is buried in the local Killeeneen Cemetery. There are statues erected to his honour in Craughwell and in Kiltimagh. A Raftery Festival – Feile Raifteiri – is held every March in Loughrea, County Galway to commemorate his poetic legacy.

Most of Raftery's poems were in the old Irish, oral tradition and were only committed to print after his death. The first President of Ireland - Douglas Hyde – as well as Lady Gregory and William Butler Yeats took an interest in his poems and created English as well as Irish versions of his work. His account of a drowning tragedy in 1828 at Annaghdown on Lough Corrib is recorded in one of his most famous poems, Eanach Dhuin.

When Mayo County Council Library ran an open competition in 2008 to discover Mayo's all-time favourite poem, Raftery's Cill Aodhain was the clear winner. The first verse is listed below.

Anois teacht an Earraigh,
beidh an lá dúl chun shíneadh,
Is tar eis na féil Bríde
ardóigh mé mo sheol.
Ó chuir mé i mo cheann é
ní chónóidh mé choíche
Go seasfaidh mé síos
i lár Chontae Mhaigh Eo

With the coming of Spring
the day will be lengthening,
and after St. Bridget's Day
I shall raise my sail.

Since I put it into my head, I shall never stay put
until I'm standing down in the centre of County Mayo.

Antoine O'Raifteiri

Lyrics of some Mayo songs

Moonlight in Mayo
(Percy Weinrich and Jack Mahoney)

It was just a year ago today I left old Erin's Isle
My heart was throbbin' in the soft light of my colleen's smile
In all my dreams I seem to hear her sweet voice soft and low
I know she's waiting where we said goodbye in old Mayo

Chorus

For two Irish eyes are shining
and an Irish heart is pining
and when I kissed her and caressed her
in the gloaming long ago
Loving Irish arms will press me
and true Irish love caress me
and sweet Irish lips will bless me
when it's Moonlight in Mayo

Her Irish eyes like beacons shine all in the darkest night
I know the sweet love beams below will always fill the world with light
the roses of her cheeks will lend enchantment to the sea
and when shamrocks wear the dew I'll wed my sweet colleen

Chorus

Westport House

Boys from the County Mayo
(Author - unknown)

Far away from the land of the Shamrock and heather
In search of a living, as exiles we roam
And whenever we chance to assemble together
We think of the land where we once had a home:
But our homes are destroyed and our soil confiscated
The hand of the tyrant brought plunder and woe;
The fires are now quenched and our hearts desolated
In our once happy homes in the County Mayo

Long years have now passed since with hearts full of sorrow
The land of the Shamrock we left far behind;
But how we would like to going back there tomorrow;
To the scenes of our youth, which we still bear in mind;
The days of our childhood, it's now we regret them
They cling to our vision wherever we go;
And the friends of our youth we shall never forget them
They too are exiled from the County Mayo

From historic Killala, from Swinford to Balla
Ballyhaunis and Westport and old Castlebar
Kiltimagh and Claremorris, Belmullet and Erris
Kilkelly and Knock that is famed near and far;
Balla, Ballina, Ballinrobe and Bohola
Keelogues and Foxford a few miles below

Newport and Cong with old Straide and Manulla
Charlestown too, in the County Mayo

So boys pull together in all kinds of weather
Don't show the white feather wherever you go
Be like a brother and love one another
Like stout hearted men from the County Mayo

Green and Red of Mayo
Author: Saw Doctors

Oh the Green and Red of Mayo
I can see it still
It's soft and craggy bogland
It's tall majestic hills
Where the ocean kisses Ireland
And the waves carress it's shore
Oh the feeling it came over me
To stay forever more, Forever more

From it's rolling coastal waters
I can see Croagh Patrick's peak
Where one Sunday every Summer
The pilgrims climb the Reek
Where Saint Patrick in his solitude
Looked down across Clew Bay
And with a ringing of his bell
Called the faithful there to pray, There to pray

Oh take me to Clare Island
The home of Granuaile
It's waters harbour fishes
From the herring to the whale
And now I must depart it
And reality is plain
May the time not pass so slowly
Before I set sail again, Set sail again

The Green and Red of Mayo
I can see it still
It's soft and craggy bogland
It's tall majestic hills
Where the ocean kisses Ireland
And the waves carress it's shore
The feeling it came over me
To stay forever more, Forever more

Kilkelly Ireland
(Peter Jones)

Kilkelly, Ireland, 18 and 60, my dear and loving son John
Your good friend the schoolmaster Pat McNamara's so good
as to write these words down.

Your brothers have all gone to find work in England,
the house is so empty and sad
The crop of potatoes is sorely infected,
a third to a half of them bad.
And your sister Brigid and Patrick O'Donnell
are going to be married in June.
Your mother says not to work on the railroad
and be sure to come on home soon.

Kilkelly, Ireland, 18 and 70, dear and loving son John
Hello to your Mrs and to your 4 children,
may they grow healthy and strong.
Michael has got in a wee bit of trouble,
I guess that he never will learn.
Because of the dampness there's no turf to speak of
and now we have nothing to burn.
And Brigid is happy, you named a child for her
and now she's got six of her own.
You say you found work, but you don't say
what kind or when you will be coming home.

Kilkelly, Ireland, 18 and 80, dear Michael and John, my sons
I'm sorry to give you the very sad news
that your dear old mother has gone.
We buried her down at the church in Kilkelly,
your brothers and Brigid were there.
You don't have to worry, she died very quickly,
remember her in your prayers.
And it's so good to hear that Michael's returning,
with money he's sure to buy land
For the crop has been poor and the people
are selling at any price that they can.

Kilkelly, Ireland, 18 and 90, my dear and loving son John
I guess that I must be close on to eighty,
it's thirty years since you're gone.
Because of all of the money you send me,
I'm still living out on my own.
Michael has built himself a fine house
and Brigid's daughters have grown.
Thank you for sending your family picture,
they're lovely young women and men.
You say that you might even come for a visit,
what joy to see you again.

Kilkelly, Ireland, 18 and 92, my dear brother John
I'm sorry that I didn't write sooner to tell you
that father passed on.
He was living with Brigid, she says he was cheerful
and healthy right down to the end.
Ah, you should have seen him play with
the grandchildren of Pat McNamara, your friend.
And we buried him alongside of mother,
down at the Kilkelly churchyard.
He was a strong and a feisty old man,
considering his life was so hard.
And it's funny the way he kept talking about you,
he called for you in the end.
Oh, why don't you think about coming to visit,
we'd all love to see you again.

Isle of Hope, Isle of Tears
Author: Brendan Graham

On the first day of January Eighteen Ninety-two
They opened Ellis Island and they let the people through.
And the first to cross the threshold
Of the Isle of hope and tears
Was Annie Moore from Ireland
Who was all of fifteen years.

Chorus

Isle of hope, Isle of tears,
Isle of freedom, Isle of fears,
But it's not the Isle I left behind...
That Isle of hunger, Isle of pain,
Isle you'll never see again
But the Isle of home Is always on your mind.

In her little bag she carried
All her past and history
And her dreams for the future In the land of liberty.
And courage is the passport
When your old world disappears
'Cause there's no future in the past
When you're fifteen years.

Chorus

When they closed down Ellis Island
In Nineteen Forty-three
Seventeen million people Had come there for sanctuary.
And in springtime when I came here
And stepped onto its piers,
I thought of how it must have been
When you're only fifteen years.

Chorus

Brendan Graham - Beyond the Half Door

I'll be happy
(Words Tom Brett, Melody Eric Bogle)

Verse 1

For close on seventy years I've followed Mayo
Of wins and draws and losses I've been through many
The county's drive for Sam has seen me laugh and cry
The good days are so good, my hopes are always high
My love for the green and red is forever in my head
Just bring Sam back home to Mayo and I'll be happy

Verse 2

We somehow lost our way after the carefree, winning fifties
Our midfield maestro Carney left when only in his twenties
The boat to Holyhead took away our players and teams
No work, no team, no September football dreams
My love for the green and red is forever in my head
Just bring Sam back home to Mayo and I'll be happy

Verse 3

The winless years then came, our young were leaving still
No flying Knock Airport then, just a bog atop a hill
With Celtic tiger days, our young stayed home instead
Our universities and colleges saw our local talent bred
My love for the green and red is forever in my head
Just bring Sam back home to Mayo and I'll be happy

Verse 4

The East coast gets first call on the infrastructure subsidies
With Mayo and the West, just the crumbs of financial droughts
But Knock Airport is flying now, our man Horan got that so right
Our new bunch of players have the strength and speed and fight
My love for the green and red is forever in my head
Just bring Sam back home to Mayo and I'll be happy

Final

For close on seventy years I've followed Mayo
Of wins and draws and losses I've been through many
The county's drive for Sam has seen me laugh and cry
The good days are so good, my hopes are always high
My love for the green and red is forever in my head
Just bring Sam back home to Mayo and I'll be happy

We are Mayo
Lyrics by Tom Brett, Arrangement by Keith Brett

I am the legend of Carney, Quinn and Prendergast
I am the great Sean Freyne, still fighting till the last
We have our hope, we have our dream
We're coming home, we're on your team
From Inisturk to Erris Head
We proudly wear the Green and Red

Chorus

We are Mayo
From Ireland's West we come
We have our hope
We have our dream
We're by your side and on your team
We are Mayo
From Ireland's West we come
From Inishturk to Erris Head
We proudly wear the Green and Red
We are Mayo

I am of Blacksod, Achill, Knock and Clare Island
I've walked the Ceide fields,
climbed the Reek and fished the Moy
From Sydney bay to Amerikay,
Cong's Quiet Man to Grainne Uaile
From Inishturk to Erris Head
We proudly wear the Green and Red

Chorus

We walked the road to Delphi
We're of the Castlebar Races
We've battled for the glory and
We've risen from the ashes
We have our hope, we have our dream
We're coming home, we're on your team
From Inishturk to Erris Head
We proudly wear the Green and Red

Chorus

We are Mayo, We are Mayo
We are Mayo, We are Mayo

Tom Brett, Keith Brett

When Darkness Falls

Ireland's first International Dark Sky Park is located right here in County Mayo. The Dark Sky Park is very large extending over 150 square kilometres and covers both the Ballycroy National Park and the Wild Nephin area in the west of the county.

For those of you who spend most of your life among the bright lights of the world's cities and towns, the opportunity to undertake some stargazing on a clear, dark night in the Mayo wilderness is an experience to be cherished and never forgotten.

The area encompassing Mayo's International Dark Sky Park has that most sought-after characteristic for star gazers – the absence of light! The opportunity to take time out and look skywards, watch the thousands of stars in our Milky Way galaxy, planets, occasional satellites and the International Space Station sailing by in the heavens, is enough to fill us all with awe and amazement. Grab the opportunity to experience nature in its rawest form and just allow yourself time to reflect on the wonder of our universe and creation itself.

You may even get lucky and see the occasional meteor shower or, if the heavenly gods are very kind, a glimpse of the Aurora Borealis. For Mayo folk, sightings of the Northern Lights can be a once in a lifetime experience and views of our own green and red aurora colours over places such as Ballycroy or Downpatrick Head an extra bonus.

Aurora from Mayo (Photo: Brian Wilson)

Dun Briste Aurora (Photo: Brian Wilson)

The International Dark Skies Gold Tier status was awarded to the Wild Nephin - Ballycroy National Park area in 2016. Much of the credit in achieving such lofty recognition must go to students at the Galway Mayo Institute of Technology under the guidance of Professor Brian Espey from Trinity College's Astro-Physics Department. Long hours of night sky surveying over many months played a critical part in reaching the Gold Tier status. Such recognition is only given to areas that exhibit exceptional night skies with magnificent nightscapes and Mayo is lucky to possess them in the sky above.

There are some strategically placed viewing platforms in the Dark Sky area including the Ballycroy Visitor Centre, the Claggan Mountain Boardwalk as well as Letterkeen Bothy. All have good road access, interpretative and parking facilities.

You will certainly sleep better after a night visit to Mayo's Dark Sky area!

Enjoy it!

Claggan Walkway to the Stars (Photo: Brian Wilson)

Letterkeen Bothy (Photo: Brian Wilson)

Noctilucent Portacloy Beach, North Mayo (Photo: Brian Wilson)

In conclusion

Our fervent desire in writing this book was to reach out to all Mayo people – those living not only in Ireland or Britain but also the very large, worldwide Mayo diaspora who for various reasons now live their lives in places far away from the county of their birth.

The title 'We are Mayo' was chosen quite deliberately. It reflects that common bond that exists between us, helps unite us and hopefully will never leave us.

When the concept of this book was being tossed about between us and a broad-brush plan was starting to emerge, we felt a great desire to produce something that we hoped would find a niche in every home and household in Mayo. Furthermore, we also hoped that local Mayo people reading the book would feel a similar desire to share a copy with fellow family members and friends all over the globe. That in a nutshell is what this 'We are Mayo' book means to us.

The design of the book is built around a simple formula incorporating sections dealing with our geographic location in the world, our history, our infrastructure, our sporting and other legends both young and old – all brought together by the great accident of our birth or choice of residence in our unique and beautiful county on the west coast of Ireland. No doubt other authors would include many other aspects of our county and its people that we have not included and probably the reverse. We've tried to keep the content as non-political and non-sectarian as we could with editorial independence a key driver in achieving this.

One of the outstanding success stories in bringing this entire project to completion has been the contributions from a long list of professional and non-professional photographers, all extremely generous with sharing their beautiful images of our county. Their collective generosity and skill have enhanced the quality of the book in a manner that the written word could never hope to achieve. We hope that for years to come your unique contributions will be acknowledged, admired and treasured by all who come to read 'We are Mayo'.

Ireland's First Lady, Sabina Higgins, has provided a fitting foreword to the book reflecting on her own childhood and adolescence in the Ballindine area of south Mayo. Being from a similar generation, we can relate to everything she has written – it is a lovely encapsulation of the days of our Mayo youth.

We are also extremely grateful to the large number of people across all walks of life who have expressed their joy and support for what 'We are Mayo' set out to achieve and how much they looked forward to the finished product. We hope all of you enjoy the book and hopefully it will become a cherished heirloom in your household for many generations to come. The entire project has given us much pleasure – it really was great fun!

Enjoy the read and the beautiful images of County Mayo!

We are Mayo!

Ceide Fields Aurora (Photo: Brian Wilson)

We are Mayo flag proudly flying in Rathmines, Dublin on All Ireland Final day 2017